imperial space

rome, constantinople and the early church

whitney

imperial space

rome, constantinople and the early church

First published in 1998 by ●●●ellipsis
55 Charlotte Road, London EC2A 3QT

Published in the United States by Whitney Library of Design,
an imprint of Watson-Guptill Publications,
a division of BPI Communications, Inc.
1515 Broadway, New York, New York 10036

ISBN 0-8230-0379-5

Designed by Jonathan Moberly
Edited by Vicky Wilson
Layout and image processing by Heike Löwenstein
Drawings by John Hewitt
Drawings on pages 210–13 generated from CAD models by
Matthew Taylor at Kent Institute of Art and Design
Glossary by Andrew Wyllie
Index by Diana LeCore
Printed and bound in Hong Kong

Library of Congress Cataloguing in Publication Data:
a catalogue record for this publication is available from the
Library of Congress

contents

Towards the end of the 1st millennium BC the authority of the Roman republic wavered. The city-state had absorbed wealthy and decadent eastern kingdoms and empires, which were governed as provinces by magistrates with unprecedented powers; venality corrupted the senate; and a state of perpetual crisis allowed the usual two consuls, replaced annually, to be superseded for long periods by ambitious individual commanders. Following the assassination of Julius Caesar in 44 BC by a faction of senators who claimed commitment to the cause of republican orthodoxy, his nephew Octavian emerged to succeed him. Accorded the title of Augustus, he promoted a return to old values and could ultimately claim to have restored the republic. From 27 BC until his death in AD 14 he was re-endowed annually with the disposal of the consulship. Called princeps (first citizen), in principle he left the senate to decide whether his accumulation of powers would survive him, but in practice he set the precedent for nominating his heir from within his family, and his adopted family name – Caesar – came to be associated with the position for ever after.

It would be difficult to overestimate the importance of Augustus in ensuring the survival of the Roman empire for some four centuries – 14 until the fall of its eastern successor – and of classical civilisation indefinitely. The effectiveness of his system depended in part on the character of the ruler, and despite the lack of a formula for legitimising the succession, over the two centuries that followed there was a remarkable line of able men: Tiberius, Claudius, Vespasian, Titus and to some extent Domitian in the 1st century AD, then Trajan, Hadrian, Antoninus Pius, Marcus Aurelius, and Septimius and Alexander Severus, whose reigns covered most of the years from AD 98 to 235. With security and sound administration sustained by the professional army and civil service, agriculture, industry and trade flourished, promoting a higher standard of living for more people than ever before, regardless of race or creed.

The succession was not unbroken, however, and its troubles took their toll under pressure from without and tension from within. Augustus advised against extending the empire beyond the Rhine, the Danube and the Syrian desert. Early in the 2nd century, however, Trajan decisively ignored this advice, both in Europe and the east. Celebrated in the great frieze that spirals up the commemorative column which once

dominated his forum in Rome,[1] his success was limited – especially in the struggle with Persia – and his
successors were subjected to the incessant strain of
fighting on widely dispersed fronts.

Moreover, the very security and prosperity within
the empire promoted provincial independence. Many
provinces had drawn civilisation from Rome and had
grown strong and wealthy in provisioning the imperial regime. Many had been wealthy and powerful kingdoms before Rome; now wealthy and powerful again,
they rediscovered their identities in an age of compla-
cency towards them, when distraction by remote frontier problems was sapping the vitality of the capital.
And in the army the Italian contingent was far out-
numbered by soldiers from the provinces – even from
the barbarian tribes it existed to combat.

The divided empire

By the middle of the 3rd century the cost of constant
conflict had undermined the economy and alienated
the tax-payer. The effort promoted the numerous commanders of increasingly barbarised legions whose
rivalries rent the empire within: the succession was at
their bidding, and they made emperors of those whose

concern to keep them satisfied overrode all else. After the frontier was pushed back nearly to Rome itself,[2] the great general Aurelian (270–75) emerged from the anarchy. He was assassinated before he could consolidate a new order, and it was another decade before Diocletian (284–305) restored an authority which provided the basis for radical reform.

Beyond the control of one man, the empire was divided and half was assigned to an associate emperor: Maximian from 287. Diocletian was dominus (lord) rather than princeps, but he shared the title Augustus with his associate and, to ease the succession as well as the burden of far-flung rule, each had an assistant Caesar: Galerius and Constantius Chlorus from 293. Under these four co-rulers (the tetrarchy) the empire was divided into four prefectures and the old provinces were replaced by 12 dioceses subdivided into new

1 **Rome, Forum of Trajan, commemorative column.**

Standing in the precinct before the temple later dedicated to the deified emperor, the column carried spiral reliefs representing the campaign which extended Roman rule beyond the Danube into what is now Romania. The emperor was interred in the chamber below the column.

2 Rome, Porta Ostiensis in the Aurelian walls, and the Mausoleum of Cestius.

The Emperor Aurelian (270–75) acted on the urgent need to defend the capital from the barbarian tribes who had recently reached as far south as the Po. His wall, finished five years after his assassination, was 19 kilometres (12 miles) in circuit, up to 4 metres (13 feet) thick and nearly 8 metres (26 feet) high, with a continuous wall walk, square towers at regular intervals (100 Roman feet –

provinces. The civil and military powers of the magistrates who had governed the old provinces were also
split, the former between the vicars and counts of the
new dioceses and provinces, the latter accorded to gen-
erals supporting them but ultimately responsible to the
dominus. Individuality and free enterprise were cur-
tailed. Rome was no longer the unique capital, and the
republican system 'restored' by Augustus – but retired
by the authoritarian Flavian dynasty founded by Vespasian – was officially dead.

After his death Augustus was interred in a mighty
mausoleum on the banks of the Tiber near the northern entrance to Rome.[3] A monument of geometrical
purity with its superimposed cylinders forming tree-

19.6 metres/64 feet) and 18 double or single gates between
twin round towers. Brick-sheathed concrete was used
throughout except for the stone-built gates. Later emperors
were responsible for considerable strengthening and
heightening exercises.

Fortuitously, relapse into the defensive mentality
characteristic of primitive societies here confronts return
to the origin of monumental stone architecture – the
pyramid. Cestius' pyramid is dated to c. 12 BC.

3 **Rome, Tomb of Augustus** 28–23 BC, as reconstructed by Gismondi in his great model of the city (Rome, Museum of Roman Civilisation).

The first emperor's tomb took the ancient Etruscan tradition of the walled tumulus (see volume 3, IMPERIAL FORM, page 104) to unprecedented proportions. Over a drum of travertine-sheathed concrete – 88 metres (289 feet) in diameter and centred on the tomb chamber – the tree-covered tumulus rises to a second drum with a tiered roof supporting a colossal bronze statue of the emperor. Many other imperial burials took place here in the 1st century AD.

4 **Rome, Tomb of Hadrian** incomplete on the emperor's death in AD 138, as reconstructed by Gismondi.

Hadrian's elaboration of the formula incorporated a podium – 84 metres (276 feet) square and 10 metres (33 feet) high – below the drum, which was 64 metres (210 feet) in diameter and contained burial chambers for the emperor and his successors. Both these elements were sheathed in marble. As an alternative to the tempietto shown rising from the tree-planted tumulus here, some restorations postulate another, smaller podium and drum. A colossal statue of Hadrian or a quadriga group crowned the whole.

5 **Rome, Tomb of Hadrian** engraving by G-B Piranesi.
The tomb was used until the death of Caracalla in 217.
Stripped of its lavish ornament, the building was converted
into a fortress (Castel Sant'Angelo) by the early medieval
popes.

planted terraces, its descent from the age-old tumulus is a tangible reminder of the antiquarian aspect of Augustan reform. In the same vein, others built pyramids (see 2, page 12). Solid mass was to cede to vaulted space as building technology advanced with concrete, but Hadrian (117–38) revived monumental mass on an unparalled scale,[4–5] and took the domed rotunda to its apogee in the Pantheon. Both were to be overwhelming in impact throughout the history of Rome and its architecture.

6 **Rome, Pantheon** c. 118, engraving of the interior by G-B Piranesi.

The realisation of the potential of concrete for the moulding of space with varied vaulting dawned with the Augustan age, the context having been provided by the engineers of the late republic in utilitarian and thermal buildings. The process began with the arch: turned on its centre, it produces the dome; extended, it becomes the tunnel (or barrel) vault; one tunnel crossed with another makes a groin over square bays defined by four arches at right angles to one another (see volume 3, IMPERIAL FORM, page 183). Subsidiary bays resist the lateral thrust of the arches, but within the sequence of the main bays the forces are counterposed, permitting the reduction of the mass of supporting masonry to relatively slender piers.

Unlike masonry, concrete is by nature a malleable material which coalesces into a homogeneous membrane. Relatively light, its weight may be reduced still further in a vault by varying the density of its aggregate – substituting pumice for stone in particular – as well as by attenuation and coffering. This was facilitated by the introduction of slower-drying mortar, so that each layer fused readily with the next, and the continuation of strictly horizontal bedding to the top instead of setting the aggregate in radial courses to form the perimeter of a dome – as in works like the Stabian Baths at Pompeii, probably dating from the last quarter of the 2nd century BC (see volume 3, IMPERIAL FORM, page 157). The final realisation of the logic of concrete structure liberated building from the limitations of traditional masonry and planning from the strictures of the rectangle. Thereafter spatial variety was to be the principal characteristic of imperial architecture.

The Pantheon

In the baths of Pompeii, domical and barrel vaults carried on heavy walls distinguish separate spaces. By the early 1st century AD, however, the crossing of barrel vaults at right angles had produced the groin, which – carried on the supports of four arches – could both let in light and allow space to flow all around. As we shall see, the spectacular spatial diversity of the great imperial thermae depends on the disposition of all three types of vault, and their central halls inspired the apotheosis of the groin vault in the last great space of imperial Rome, the Basilica of Maxentius (see 36, pages 88–89). Meanwhile, the apotheosis of the dome – and of space as the prime concern of architects – distinguished the Pantheon,[6–8] Hadrian's great circular tem-

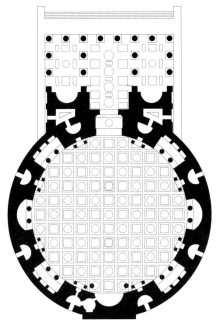

7 **Rome, Pantheon** plan.

8 **Rome, Pantheon** exterior with portico and (OVERLEAF) detail of structure.

Central to the new district laid out by Agrippa in the peninsula formed by the bend in the Tiber to the west of the Capitoline, the original Pantheon was dedicated early in Augustus' principate, destroyed with most of its patron's other monuments in the great fire of AD 80, rebuilt by Domitian, evidently in its original form, and destroyed again in 110. Hadrian's work, begun c. 118 and completed a decade later, was entirely new. The inscription on the frieze of the pedimented portico, crediting it to Agrippa, has led most to conclude that this element was reused, especially as it is so ill related to the great rotunda which forms the body of the building. Scientific analysis does not support this view, however, and it is now generally thought that the inscription was replaced in due honour to the original founder. The colonnaded forecourt would effectively have framed the portico, largely masking the curved walls of the rotunda. The exterior was divided into three registers but was otherwise plain – except, of course, for the stone portico which once carried sculpture groups.

The drum – 43.2 metres (142 feet) in diameter – is based on a concrete ring 4.5 metres (15 feet) deep and more than twice as wide. The superstructure diminishes in thickness

from just over 6 metres (20 feet) in the drum to just over 1.5 metres (5 feet) at the rim of the oculus (though masonry sheathing was needed to perfect the hemispherical profile of the dome, masking the junction of the true intrados with the heightened drum). The grading of the aggregate from basalt at the base to pumice at the top, together with the coffering, are crucial in further lightening the load. This reduction of weight permitted the alternation of the exedrae and aedicules, but within the plastic mass of concrete above the former (and other hidden cavities), relieving arches of brick deflect the pressure of the dome to the intermediate piers.

The two registers of the drum had a revetment of vari-coloured marble. Red and grey Egyptian granite columns, nearly 12 metres (40 feet) high, screened the exedrae, countering the entrance axis and deflecting the eye into the once-stuccoed dome.

9 **Pergamon, sanctuary of Asclepius** mid 2nd century, brick-vaulted rotunda crypt.

The Pantheon was often to be emulated, perhaps first on a relatively small scale in the Temple of Asclepius and the crypt of its neighbouring rotunda at Pergamon. The lack of suitable ingredients for concrete in the eastern provinces inhibited the development of an architecture of space on the metropolitan model. Materials were ultimately to be imported, but at first brick was pressed into service, as at Pergamon. The form of the large rotunda was new, but the tradition of the grand brick vault goes back to ancient Mesopotamia (see volume 1, ORIGINS, page 56).

ple to all the gods, while the greatest of barrel vaults canopied the throne of the emperor himself.

The Pantheon's great rotunda, built by Hadrian on the site of the rectilinear temple founded by Augustus' general Agrippa, was unprecedented in scale. Built mainly of concrete, the temple consists of a cylindrical drum topped by a hemispherical dome so that the weight of the latter, lightened in substance, structure and form, is transmitted directly to the ground through the former. Exedrae 'excavated' from the perimeter mass, enhancing its monumentality by revealing its depth while at the same time further lightening the load on the foundations, accommodate the principal deities. As the drum is half the height of its diameter, the dome – encapsulating conceptually the sphere of heaven embracing all the gods – rises to a height equal to the diameter. The Pantheon has rarely been equalled for size and durability: it has survived virtually intact to inspire architects for nearly 2000 years.[9]

Secular building

It was Roman secular building, with its much more varied requirements, that took the lead in the diversification of space. Augustus' residence on the Palatine was modest, and little of detail is known of his successor's more extensive Domus Tiberiana. More survives of the palaces of Nero and Domitian, however, which set standards to be emulated by princely builders ever after. Domitian's Domus Augustana had the largest ceremonial spaces yet covered and the most sophisticated of private apartments, but nothing that excelled Nero's most stunning achievement, the main reception room in the Domus Aurea.

Whatever their shortcomings as rulers, both Nero (54–68) and Domitian (81–96) rank among the greatest patrons of architecture. Both were responsible for extensive rebuilding after devastating fires, Nero notoriously expropriating a considerable amount of the wasted area for his own purposes but Domitian following the lines originally developed by Agrippa, at least in the area around the Pantheon. As well as markets and sporting facilities, Nero provided a magnificent and much-needed thermal complex to supplement the Baths of Agrippa. Domitian built temples and a new forum beside that of Augustus and followed Nero with a new stadium on the Campus Martius. And both were to leave indelible imprints on the history of architecture with their palaces.

The Domus Augustana

Domitian's stadium and forum were conservative – marking the end of development in the old tradition of limited internal space and elaborate external form – but his palace, begun by the architect Rabirius early in his reign, had rooms of unprecedented scale and variety.[10] The site on the Palatine was divided between public ceremonial to the west, with ready access from the forum below, and private retreat to the east. The disparate characters of the two parts were uncompromisingly manifest in their distribution and massing:

10 **Rome, Domus Augustana** inaugurated in 92, plan and (OVERLEAF) reconstructed perspective of the main state rooms.

The official imperial residence on the Palatine was built by the architect Rabirius over the first ten years of the reign of the third Flavian emperor, Domitian, and extended eastwards over terraces beyond the stadium-shaped garden by Septimius Severus (193–211). Officially known as the Domus Augustana (but popularly called Palatium and therefore giving its name to the genre of great palaces descended from it), it eclipsed the earlier imperial residences on the site.

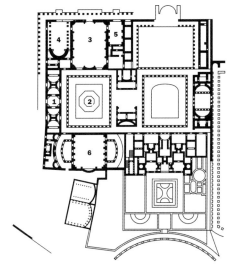

The palace of Tiberius, which itself had eclipsed that of Augustus to the west of a saddle in the hill, was adapted to provide grand access from the forum below. The new work, sited to the east of the saddle, was designed to provide for public ceremonial as well as private retreat. The state rooms were built partly on terraces over the falling ground towards

the west, where they were served by the road running up
through the declivity, and also communicated with the
Domus Tiberiana; the private apartments were secured to
the east, where they communicated with the imperial box
overlooking the Circus Maximus.

The public entrance to the palace from the forum opened
into a vestibule unprecedented in its dimensions – 33 metres
(109 feet) by 24.5 metres (80 feet) – as a covered space,
except by the greatest of Rabirius' works on the Palatine
above. Beyond this was a guard room and the ramp which
tacked back and forth up to the Domus Tiberiana. Over the
declivity and its road, the entrance (1) to the ceremonial
quarters was a domed pavilion in the centre of a range of
varied spaces fronting the central peristyle (2) but also from
an outer portico which bent around the northern corner.
To the north of the peristyle were the hall of audience
(3, aula regia, 29 metres/95 feet wide), the neighbouring
aisled basilica (4, the imperial seat of justice, 14.5 metres/
48 feet wide) and the much smaller chapel (5, lararium).
To the south, the state banqueting room (6, triclinium) was
29 metres (95 feet) wide. Unbuttressed but colonnaded
towards the central peristyle and the twin fountain courts,
the banqueting room must have had a flat ceiling.

Entered from the south in the centre of a concave portico

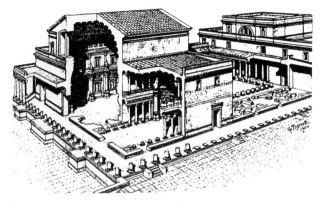

flanking the Circus Maximus, the private wing was
arranged on two floors beside the stadium-shaped garden
(incomplete on Domitian's death) and around a garden
court. The upper level communicated with the ceremonial
block through a second peristyle to the north-east, close
to the centre of the complex as a whole. Between court
and peristyle, the main range of the private apartments
had an axis of loggias and halls between two similar suites
overlooking the garden court and backed by loggias facing
the peristyle.

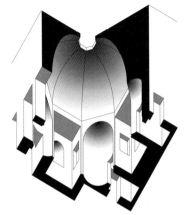

11 **Rome, Domus Augustana** rooms opening off the garden court, axonometric, section and plan.

The properties of concrete were exploited for still richer spatial variety here: two of the rooms were domed octagons with alternately apsidal and rectangular spaces carved from the sides. The apsidal recessions imply the principle of the squinch (an arch thrown across the corners of a square space to support the rim of a dome) which was to be widely employed in the development of spatial architecture.

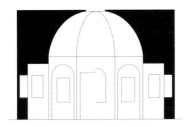

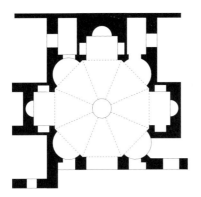

the intricate rooms of the main private apartments looked south from two levels over a garden court; the imperious hall of audience, basilica and chapel addressed the state banqueting room over the colonnaded entrance court.

The nature of the vaulting over the ceremonial rooms – indeed whether there were vaults at all over the larger ones – is open to question. It is usually accepted that the chapel could easily have been vaulted and that the colonnaded basilica had a flat ceiling with a semi-dome over the apse where the emperor sat. However, there is less readiness to agree that these lateral structures could have buttressed a great barrel vault over the hall of audience: the supposition is supported by the ambitiousness of Domitian and Rabirius as well as by evidence of strain in the partition walls, despite their great mass. The piers dividing the hall of audience internally into bays were framed by colossal marble columns echoing those on either side of the niche for the imperial throne which terminated the main longitudinal axis.

Heavy barrel vaults would have admitted light only at the ends, of course. The infusion of space with light depends on the lightening of structure in response to the lightening of load – especially in its distribution to isolated points. Rabirius could manage that too: excavation in the lower level of the Domus Augustana's private apartments has revealed octagonal rooms surrounded by alternating rectangular and semi-circular spaces with a dazzling array of canopy, barrel and semi-domical vaults.[11]

The Domus Aurea

In all essentials, Rabirius' garden rooms anticipate the Pantheon (see 6, page 18) on a tiny scale. Later variations are numerous: the so-called Temple of Minerva Medica is a relatively simple one from late in the imperial period.[12] The earliest and most complex example known to us, however, has been identified as the principal reception room of Nero's Domus Aurea, built c. 65 by the architects Severus and Celer.

A villa-like palace built in the centre of Rome on the site below the Palatine where the Colosseum now stands, the Domus Aurea[13] set a standard of opulence rarely surpassed. Addressing an artificial lake, the great recession in its main façade stamped it as a grand variation on the form of the seaside villa (see 15, page 42) – incongruous in the principal urban residence

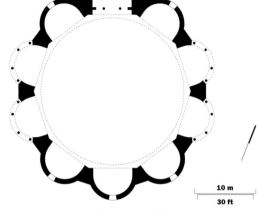

12 **Rome, so-called Temple of Minerva Medica** early 4th century, plan and perspective of original structure.

This decagonal pavilion in the Licinian gardens was possibly a tomb. Of its nine apses, the one opposite the colonnaded entrance was slightly deeper than the others and the pairs half way round on each side were also colonnaded to extend the transverse axis. The concrete forming the decagonal dome was laid in courses separated horizontally by tiles and vertically by brick ribs. In similar structures it

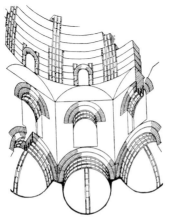

has been observed that the lack of a developed relationship
between the ribs and the piers between the arches below
denies the former the primary structural role of distributing
the load of the vault. Indeed, the ribs seem to have risen
with the vault rather than as a preconceived structural
frame; like the tiles, their purpose seems to have been to
localise settlement as the concrete dried. Several of the ribs
here survived long after the concrete fell, leaving an
impression of structural virility not lost on later builders.

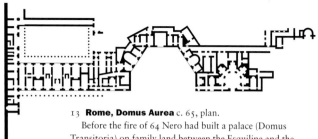

13 Rome, Domus Aurea c. 65, plan.

20 m
60 ft

Before the fire of 64 Nero had built a palace (Domus Transitoria) on family land between the Esquiline and the Palatine, deflecting the line of the Via Sacra. Swept away in the clearance after the fire, what little remained to be incorporated in the foundations of the Temple of Venus and Rome indicates considerable spatial variety – in particular a rotunda in a cross with groin-vaulted arms.

After the fire the land to the east of the Domus Transitoria was sequestered and added to Nero's estate to provide the setting for his new palatial villa, the Domus Aurea. At the end of the Via Sacra, by the site of the Domus Transitoria, the three wings of a colonnaded propylaeum framed a colossal statue of the emperor. After his assassination the artificial lake gave way to the Colosseum, the palace itself disappeared under the platform of the Baths of Titus and the propylaeum under that of the Temple of Venus and Rome.

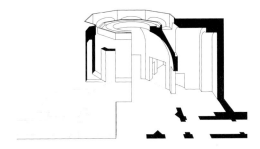

14 **Rome, Domus Aurea** main reception room, axonometric.

The enigma of the main reception room has fascinated its visitors ever since it was rediscovered early in the 16th century: solid but void; centrifugal in form but centripetal in effect; dazzling engineering but incompletely resolved geometry (the awkward little triangles between the subsidiary spaces have not escaped censure); sophisticated yet unprecedented. Buried under later building and detritus, it was one of the 'grottos' in which Raphael and his circle discovered the antique mode of decoration.

of the head of state – and its expansive park, won from sequestered land, certainly made it no more acceptable.

The main reception room, addressing the park, consisted of an octagon surrounded by an ambulatory with rectangular spaces opening from its inner sides.[14] The octagon had a canopy vault springing from the imposts of an arcade surrounding the ambulatory; the subsidiary spaces are alternately barrel and groin vaulted. Space was moulded not only by virtuoso concrete work but by light: a central oculus admitted a strong shaft of light to the main chamber; the lunettes formed by the arches rising above the main chamber's canopy admitted moderate and relatively uniform light to the ambulatory which was borrowed as a dim glow by the inner chambers.

The villas of Tiberius and Hadrian

It is no accident that the most daring example of Roman vaulting known to us occurred in a villa-like palace. In contrast with the extreme formality of distribution about atrium and peristyle typical of the greatest town houses in the imperial period, the villa was informal, rich in spatial variety, extroverted in aspect and sensitive to the natural qualities of its site. After a long line of Campanian examples, Tiberius set an imperial standard of secluded integration with nature in his retreat on Capri.[15] Later the younger Pliny provided detailed descriptions of his own several country and seaside villas, now lost. Spatial variety was the key, with the principal rooms projecting from the main mass to embrace garden or view, and loggias – covered verandah-like spaces, screened to the outside only by columns – effecting the transition from interior to exterior.

The greatest representative of the type is Hadrian's villa at Tivoli.[16] Laid out at the scale of a town, its stunning variety of buildings included forums and baths as well as reception and living rooms. Except for the Great Baths, which had impressive groin vaults, the patron's prime interest was not in the grandeur of covered space but in intimacy. Here curve and counter-curve are woven into the most intricate of forms, a few daringly vaulted, many open to the sky, some introverted, others extroverted in aspect, but all related to one another informally in accordance with the contours of the site – recalling the sensitivity of the Greeks, for whom Hadrian had a particular affinity.

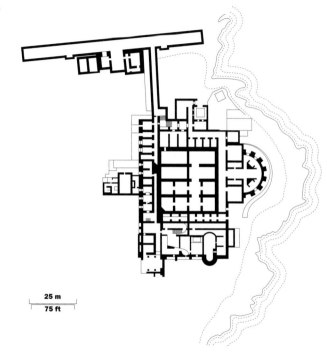

25 m
75 ft

15 **Capri, Villa Jovis** c. 25–35, plan.

Capri was originally developed by Augustus. The Villa
Jovis, the retreat of the Emperor Tiberius, was built on
terraces over the eastern cliffs high above the sea and
comprised four wings relatively informally related to one
another on different levels around a rectangular court built
over a water reservoir. The largest and lowest wing, to
the south, contained the entrance and baths. Rooms for
attendants were stacked on three storeys to the west.
The imperial apartments were isolated from the rest of the
complex in the east and north wings: the main state room
projected out over the cliff to the east, embracing the view
of the sea; the emperor's personal accommodation occupied
the highest ground to the north, with views from a loggia
over the Bay of Naples and a ramp leading down to an
elongated terrace facing in the same direction and centred
on the dining room.

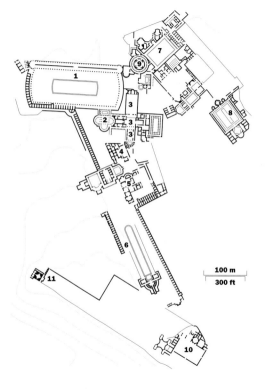

16 **Tivoli, Hadrian's Villa** c. 125–37, plan and model (OVERLEAF).

(1) Entrance and 'Poikile'; (2) triclinium; (3) stadium; (4) Small Baths; (5) Great Baths; (6) 'Canopus'; (7) private apartments; (8) Piazza d'Oro; (9) 'Teatro Marittimo' retreat; (10) academy; (11) 'Roccabruna' belvedere.

In extending a vast array of buildings over a considerable tract of countryside, Hadrian was probably emulating Domitian, who augmented several existing villas with much new work in the great estate he amassed between Albano, Castel Gandolfo and the Via Appia. In incorporating facilities for sport, study and entertainment – gymnasia, libraries, theatres, galleries – Domitian himself was following the lead set by the magnates of the late republic. In accordance with a well-established conceit, the titles given to several of the major elements of Hadrian's complex refer to famous places elsewhere: for instance, 'Canopus' recalls the sanctuary of Canopus outside Alexandria; 'Poikile' the painted stoa of the stoic philosophers at Athens.

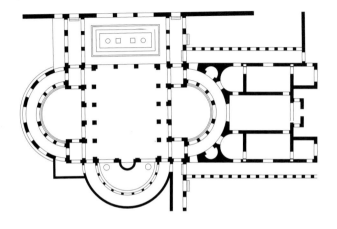

17 Tivoli, Hadrian's Villa, triclinium plan.

The main space, with its three exedrae, may have had a timber ceiling.

Immediately beyond the entrance court, the so-called triclinium[17] was the reception room where the emperor received the acclamation due to his semi-divine nature. The place of epiphany, it descended from the royal vestibules of the Hellenistic east, themselves descended from the tent of appearance of campaigning monarchs from time immemorial. The heb-sed festival tent of the Egyptian pharaoh, expanded to a monumental scale for the great hall of Tuthmosis III at Karnak (see volume 1, ORIGINS, page 131), is the most potent witness to this tradition. The bit-hilani of the Hittites and their heirs is another permutation, flanked by towers symbolic of super-human power (see volume 1, ORIGINS, page 213). The columned halls of the Urartians and Achaemenids are hardly less relevant (see volume 1, ORIGINS, pages 216–17). The Ptolemies, Hellenistic rulers of Egypt, modelled themselves on the pharaoh, of course, and the Seleucids, contemporary rulers of western Asia, on the Achaemenids and their Syrian predecessors. Ptolemaic or Seleucid, the prototype for Hadrian's vestibule has disappeared, but it is doubtless recorded in the Roman fastigium, a portico whose canopy-like image we encountered on the sides of Tiberius' Arch at Orange

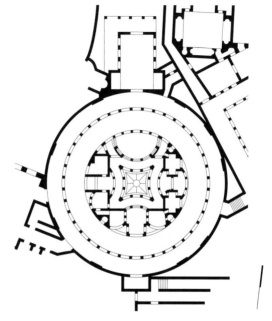

18 **Tivoli, Hadrian's Villa, 'Teatro Marittimo'** plan.

19 **Tivoli, Hadrian's Villa, 'Teatro Marittimo'** overview
into the moated fountain court.

The degree to which this complex was roofed remains
controversial. On the 'island' beyond the unroofed moat all
may well have been roofed except the central fountain
court, whose curved colonnades echo those terminating the
main spaces, allowing for the transmission of light to the
depths of the exceptionally complex conception.

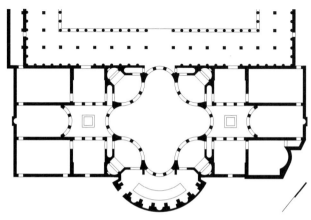

20 **Tivoli, Hadrian's Villa, Piazza d'Oro complex** plan.

21 **Tivoli, Hadrian's Villa, Piazza d'Oro** entrance pavilion.

The entrance pavilion recalls that of the Domus Augustana and the garden rooms of the private apartments there, with their alternately rectangular and semi-circular exedrae (see 11, pages 32–33). Resembling an umbrella, the dome springs from the imposts of the arches over the recessions, without a rim – let alone a drum. The squinch is anticipated, as in the Flavian prototypes.

in anticipation of the monumental reality at Baalbek (see volume 3, IMPERIAL FORM, pages 226 and 221).

Deep within the complex, the 'Teatro Marittimo'[18-19] was an exceptionally intricate and intimate retreat, and the Piazza d'Oro[20] provided for the appearance of the super-human monarch among the most select of men. The domical entrance pavilion here[21] is another manifestation of the tradition of palace vestibules inherited by the Seleucids from their predecessors in Syria and Mesopotamia: symbolising the canopy of heaven, this form achieved its early apotheosis on the Ziggurat of Nanna at Ur (see volume 1, ORIGINS, pages 72–73). Adapted to the tent of appearance, it became the ciborium or baldacchino, the domical canopy ubiquitously carried over thrones and altars. It prompts the arching of the entablature over the central bay of the typical fastigium, it is echoed in the great niche above the palatial portal and, taken to decorative extreme, it appears in many variations on the theme of the palace in the frescoes of Pompeii (see volume 3, IMPERIAL FORM, pages 168–69). Hadrian's Piazza d'Oro pavilion was doubtless directly inspired by the main entrance to the Domus Augustana (see 10, page 31), though in the later

22 **Tivoli, Hadrian's Villa, Small Baths** elongated
'octagonal' room.

The space is vaulted over a daringly undulating perimeter
not unlike that of the main interior space of the Piazza
d'Oro complex.

work the external mass follows the form of the interior space.

The complex at the head of the Piazza d'Oro enshrined the ultimate scene of imperial epiphany, the throne room. Given Hadrian's antiquarian interests, particularly his quotations from Ptolemaic Egypt, the precedent is doubtless a lost Hellenistic one. Considerable speculation persists over whether the undulating colonnades, alternately concave and convex and forming a partially double-skinned quatralobe, could have carried a vault like that of the 'octagonal' room in the Small Baths.[22] If so, the transformation of the tent of appearance in accordance with the symbolism of heaven could hardly have been more clearly articulated.

Roman baths

Roman experiments with the diversification of space culminate in the great thermae built all over the empire by successive emperors vying for prestige[23] – and expanding the vault types and mortared rubble construction techniques crucial for the future development of architecture in east and west alike. Unlike the Pompeian baths, the imperial thermae of the 2nd and

3rd centuries were distinguished by the development of an axial approach to planning ultimately in tune with the natural line of progression in the bathing process from cool to hot and back again. From the entrance and changing rooms, many would go first for a plunge in the pool of the cold zone (frigidarium), then on through a tepid chamber (tepidarium) to the hot zone (calidarium), best placed on the southern side. Alternatively one could go straight from the changing rooms through the tepid zone to the hot rooms and then, perhaps, back through the tepid zone for a swim in the pool.

Despite a strong axis, this progression is not yet apparent in the Roman Baths of Titus (c. 80): here the entrance seems to have been through the hot zone to the south, forcing the user to proceed in the opposite sense to the bathing process. In the next great complex of which there are significant traces, the Baths of Trajan (c. 109), plan and process are developed in accord: the entrance is from the north, with the hot zone to the south beyond the great groin-vaulted cen-

23 OVERLEAF **Mactris (modern Maktar, Tunisia), Great Baths** late 2nd century, view into palaestra.

tral hall which fulfilled a social function as a meeting place as well as providing a tepid zone of transition. This concourse has disappeared, but the great hall of the market building above Trajan's Forum provides a parallel – indeed, it is the earliest surviving example of such a structure on such a scale.[24]

The type culminated in the Baths of Caracalla[25] of c. 210 and those built by Diocletian some 80 years later (see 28, page 70). Paired changing rooms, presumably for men and women, on either side of the northern entrance lead sideways to the outdoor swimming pool or forwards through a central hall with cold-water troughs and a vestibule with tepid ones to the hot-water room and adjoining steam chambers in the south. The opening of a lateral axis through the hall provides for exercise in palaestrae in addition to bathing. Outside the main building, the compound contained fields for athletics and an arena for racing. Around the perimeter there were meeting and reception rooms and libraries, as well as massage parlours and shops.

In each of these two vast complexes, organised around the simple principle of choice presented by two lines of development, the spaces aligned on the

24 **Rome, Trajan's Forum, market building** c. 100.

The central hall – 28 by 9.8 metres (92 by 32 feet) and
12 metres (40 feet) high – was similar, no doubt, to the
tepidarium of the Baths of Trajan and provided a model
for the future.

25 **Rome, Baths of Caracalla** dedicated in 216, plan and model (OVERLEAF).

(1) Entrances from the north; (2) swimming pool (natatio); (3) central hall with troughs of cold water (frigidarium); (4) vestibule with troughs of tepid water (tepidarium); (5) hot-water room (calidarium); (6) palaestrae.

After the troubled generation following the death of Marcus Aurelius in 180, Septimius Severus and his successors addressed the urgent need to repair many existing buildings and provide the ever-expanding population with new bath houses. By far the greatest of these were the Baths of Caracalla, the second ruler of the line. Unlike the earlier imperial thermae, except the Great Baths of Hadrian's Villa, Caracalla's complex survives in substantial part – some of the walls of the main block of 214 by 110 metres (702 by 361 feet) still rise to their full height, though most of the vaulting has gone. The model was obviously the Baths of Trajan (built by Apollodorus of Damascus and dedicated in 109) – both for the vast compound, bordered by libraries, meeting and reception rooms, and the internal distribution of the main block to the north, with a three-bay central hall. The calidarium recalls the Pantheon – their diameters were 35 metres (115 feet) and 42.5 metres (140 feet) respectively

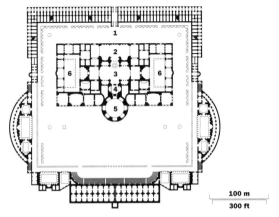

100 m
300 ft

– but the later work was taller and lit by arched windows
in the drum. Only on this side of the main block did the
regular repetition of colonnaded openings around the great
rotunda and to either side of it lend significant relief to the
massive walls. Shops masked the entrance front framing the
compound to the north, the curved side of the stadium was
flanked by a huge reservoir on the southern side and halls
with oval vestibules were accommodated in semi-circular
recessions off-centre on the other two sides.

26 **Rome, Baths of Caracalla** octagonal chamber with
dome carried on pendentives.

The pendentive is one key to the construction of a dome
over a polygonal space. Naturally the dome rests on the
centres of the straight sides, which will be pierced with
arches if the space is integrated with its context. One
solution to the problem of supporting the dome over the
corners is to throw extra arches across them (squinches) –
as in the garden rooms of the Domus Augustana (see 11,
pages 32–33) or the entrance pavilion to the Piazza d'Oro
of Hadrian's Villa (see 21, page 53). Another is to proceed as
though building two domes, the lower one springing from
the imposts of the arches defining the space. The lower
dome will be obliterated in the main by those arches and
the upper dome. Remaining between these elements, where
they diverge, are four spherical triangles – fragments of the
larger, lower dome. These are the pendentives.

27 **Recipe for a pendentive dome.**

Take a grapefruit, cut it in half, set it aside. Take a melon, cut it in half, slice off the top of one half to the diameter of the grapefruit. Slice vertically to form a square. Place the grapefruit on the residue of the melon, which represents the pendentives.

main and subsidiary axes were varied in shape and vaulting to great scenographic effect. Caracalla's architect made considerable play with curved forms and was clearly inspired by the Pantheon (see 6, page 18) for the climax of his building in the calidarium. His curved vaults usually rested on curved walls, but there is at least one example of a domical vault over a polygonal space: with great importance for the future, semi-spherical triangular elements called pendentives bridge the gap between the circular and angular surfaces.[26-27] The great groin-vaulted bays of the central halls admitted light through lunettes high above the surrounding chambers. Caracalla's hall has gone, but the core of Diocletian's complex,[28] complete with some of its original colossal Egyptian granite columns, survives as the church of S Maria degli Angeli.[29]

Decoration

With diversity of space went exuberance of decoration, with adventurousness fantasy. As concrete freed form from the constraints imposed by traditional materials, it also freed the decorative imagination from the constraints of traditional logic. In the dra-

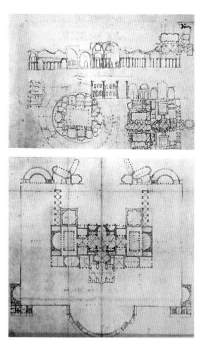

28 **Rome, Baths of Diocletian** c. 298, with Baths of Agrippa after restoration by Domitian, plans and sections sketched by Palladio.

Emulating Caracalla's complex, but less supple in plan and more restrained in its spatial variety, the main block of the Baths of Diocletian is still larger – 240 by 144 metres (787 by 472 feet). Instead of a domed rotunda at the culmination of the progression along the main axis, the calidarium echoes the three-bay central hall on a smaller scale, with apses in the centre of each side. The vista along the lateral axis was enhanced by inserting colonnaded screens between the palaestrae and the grid of inner chambers. Circular forms come to the fore as exedrae in the outer perimeter, but the symmetry with which the elements are disposed is somewhat mechanical, especially on the eastern and western sides.

29 OVERLEAF **Rome, Baths of Diocletian** central hall.

The well-preserved hall was converted into the church of S Maria degli Angeli, initially in the 16th century by Michelangelo – who disposed the altar at the end of the short axis, opposite the entrance from a vestibule formed by the tepidarium – then in the 18th century by Vanvitelli, who removed the altar to the east end of the long axis.

matic light of plastic space, the articulation of the forces implicit in masonry mass was seen to be irrelevant. Furthered by the natural propensity towards convolution – and the countering of expectation – the process goes back to the origins of the fourth style of decoration found at Pompeii, and the fashion was doubtless led by the lost precedents for the octagonal room in the Domus Aurea.

On vaults stucco remained the most popular material, at least for smaller-scale works.[30] Though sometimes used to relieve large-scale coffering with large-scale motifs, it was more often moulded with great delicacy into the frames of painted panels, carved into figures – divine, human, animal or ambivalent – and spun into webs of stylised foliage and ephemeral architecture, as in the third Pompeian style (see volume 3, IMPERIAL FORM, pages 238–39). Often bizarre in detail, this type of decoration was first rediscovered by Raphael and other artists of the Italian Renaissance in cavernous, subterranean remains (called *grottesche* after the Italian for cave).

The vaults of the Pompeian baths were stuccoed (see volume 3, IMPERIAL FORM, page 159), but plaster does not lend itself to humid environments, or intricate

30 **Rome, Via Latina, Tomb of the Anicii** 2nd century.
The ephemeral architecture of the lunettes feigns the
articulation of walls as in the Tomb of the Caetennii.

31 **Rome, Vatican cemetery, Tomb of the Caetennii**
2nd century.

Continuing the Etruscan tradition of elaborate provision
for the burial of the ashes of the cremated in urns, the
Romans built freestanding tombs within which the recession

detail to vaults on the scale of those in the imperial thermae. Mosaic was more suitable there: in marble on floors, marble and glass on walls, glass on vaults. With the proliferation of glass tesserae, structure was dissolved: as engineering became more daring, physical reality was denied. The implications were to be profound.

At the beginning of the imperial period marble was still rare in Italy, even for revetment. However, the imi-

housing the main patron's urn was distinguished by an aedicule as Hellenisation advanced. By the middle of the 2nd century aedicules had proliferated in a decorative band broken only by a great arched niche to distinguish the main one – often above an arcaded podium in which the elongated cavities accommodated full burials. The aedicules flanking the central one here had half pediments: this motif appeared in late Pompeii, but features most prominently on the hemicyclical façade of Trajan's market building.

By the end of the 2nd century inhumation had replaced cremation in Rome. Richly carved sarcophagi were the result, and rich fresco or mosaic embellished the plane surfaces of tomb walls around the elongated cavities designed to accommodate coffins.

tation of polychrome panelling in fresco was characteristic of the first style of Pompeian ornament, reflecting Hellenistic taste in the eastern provinces of the empire. Under Augustus, when marble began to replace travertine in the structure and decoration of more important buildings, it either articulated – even provided – structure or was laid in geometric patterns of contrasting colours. As the 1st century progressed and the logic of concrete superseded that of masonry, the Carrara quarries were developed and marble became more common. Free-flowing atectonic motifs ramped in intricate marble inlay or mosaic over the floors and wall surfaces of intimate spaces, but architecture long held its own in marble or plaster in grander ones.[31]

The baroque moulding of mass

The exteriors of brick and concrete buildings like the thermae rarely revealed the complexities within – even the Pantheon's third external register denies the inner nature of the dome and its relationship to the drum (see 8, page 22). Individual complexities, like the main reception room of Nero's Domus Aurea (see 14, page 39) or the garden rooms of Domitian's Domus Augustana (see 11, pages 32–33), were encapsulated within walls – often at the cost of producing dead space. The domed octagon at the entrance to the Piazza d'Oro of Hadrian's Villa (see 21, page 53) marks a significant departure towards matching space and volume in the way it stands free with all its spatial complexity expressed openly in the mass. Thereafter, indeed, the moulding of space had its counterpart in the moulding of mass into dynamic forms, not necessarily expressing the nature of the interior.

As far afield as Capua[32] and Petra, the game was admirably played by the designers of tombs – always a genre foreign to constraint. Walls undulate, concave and convex curves counter one another with dramatic effect. At Petra,[33] significantly, the pediment is broken not by the architect's mere whim to deny structural logic, but by the emotive vitality with which the central bay and its pavilion burst forth, contrary to the nature of stone. To heighten the sense of movement and the excitement of the climax, moreover, a progression was developed in the weight of the Order from sides to centre. But the game was not confined to the world of the dead.

If the outside of the theatre provided the main con-

text for the perfection of the architectonic approach to decoration, the scenae frons behind the stage inside was the ideal place to appeal to the emotions through the development of a dramatic sense of movement. The well-preserved one at Bosra well illustrates the introduction of a concave curve to amplify the orchestration of a crescendo in the centre of multiple colonnades, once richly inhabited by statuary.[34]

Beyond the theatre, the first truly spatial type of classical antiquity was the basilica, and all over the empire basilicas proliferated with increasing grandeur and variety.[35] The last great space of imperial Rome was the basilica whose ruins dominate the Via Sacra as it leads into the Forum Romanum: built by Diocletian's successors, it is sometimes called after each of

32 **Capua, 'La Conocchia' Mausoleum** late 2nd century.

In a radical development of the old formula of drum and podium with cross-reference to the eastern tomb tower, the elements are articulated as a tempietto over a high podium representing the typical aediculed burial chamber, as in the Tomb of the Caetennii (see 31, page 76), turned inside out – the niche distinguishing the main aedicule in counterplay with the tempietto.

33 Petra, 'el-Deir' Mausoleum 2nd century.

Petra was the capital of the Nabataeans, whose kingdom
– based on controlling the trade routes between Syria and
Arabia – was extinguished by Trajan in 106. Its wealth is
most tangibly recalled by the astonishing series of tombs
carved into the red sandstone cliffs – though whether the
most elaborate ones were excavated before or after the city's
annexation by the empire is controversial.

Unrelated in exterior and interior form, the tombs range
from the representation of the tower type common in the
east, with or without a veneer of classical ornament, to the
free superimposition of classical building types reproduced
in three dimensions on a colossal scale. Here the temple, the
tempietto (and ciborium) and the triumphal arch are all in
the mix – and, whether or not the Nabataeans were aping
the fashion in imperial Rome, so too is the aedicular burial
chamber turned inside out (complete with half pendentives).

34 OVERLEAF Bosra, theatre 2nd century, view from
upper cavea colonnade to tri-apsidal scenae frons.

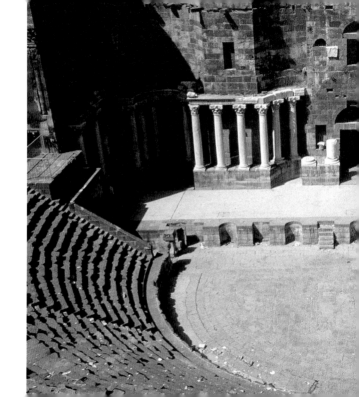

35 Trier, aula regia of the imperial palace restored interior.

Trier was the base of Constantius Chlorus, Diocletian's deputy in the west from 293. Completed under Constantius' son and successor, Constantine, the palace replaced the command headquarters destroyed when Trier was sacked by Germanic tribes in 275. Subsequently incorporated into the bishop's palace, the front and east wall have been reconstructed.

them – Maxentius who began it, Constantine who completed it. Three great groin-vaulted bays rise above barrel-vaulted side bays to admit light to the core, fusing its interrelated spaces into a whole much greater than their sum. Even as a ruin its impact was to prove inescapable.[36]

Colossal scale, scenographic alignment of varied spaces, theatrical movement in mass, complexity of planning, dramatic lighting, illusionism, rich materials – all of which we have seen in Roman imperial building from Nero's Domus Aurea to Hadrian's Villa, from the Pantheon to the great thermae and basilicas

Built of brick and roofed in timber, the aula regia – 29 by 58 metres (95 by 190 feet) – was one of the largest spaces in the colonies. To the south of the great rectangular hall was a colonnaded court and a transverse hall (narthex), to the north a generous apse. The severe exterior was plastered and relieved only by timber galleries below the windows. The now equally austere interior once had a revetment of marble. The windows of the apse are lower and smaller than those of the hall, but the eye, expecting consistency, sees the extension as greater than its physical reality. Illusionism of this kind is unmatched by the accidents of survival in Rome.

– were to be the main techniques of the Roman baroque 1500 years later. Meanwhile, the arcades and vaults of the baths and basilicas dominating Rome and its colonial towns were of prime inspiration to the builders of the so-called Middle Ages: in the east they favoured domes; in the west Romanesque architects emulated the barrel vaults, but also transmitted to their gothic followers an understanding of the principle of the counter-opposition of forces so spendidly demonstrated by the groin-vaulted central bays of the Baths of Diocletian and the great basilica built by his successors on the Via Sacra.

36 PREVIOUS PAGES **Rome, Basilica of Maxentius.**
Begun by the Emperor Maxentius (306–12), this enormous work was completed by the victorious Constantine in 312. The central hall – 80 by 25 metres (262 by 82 feet) and 35 metres (115 feet) high – was originally to be entered from the east opposite an apse to the west, but Constantine's architect opened the central barrel-vaulted bay of the south side to a porch opposite a new apse in the north.

Among the major disasters suffered by the empire before the advent of Diocletian was the defeat of the Emperor Valerian by Shapur I, of the Sassanian line, in 259.[37] Shapur's father Ardashir I, grandson of Sasan, prince of Fars, had wrested Persia from the Parthians between 224 and 226. The Parthian architectural legacy to the Sassanians was ultimately to pass to the Arabs and inform the architecture of Islam.

Parthia first appears in inscriptions of the Achaemenid king Darius I (521–486 BC) as a province of his Persian empire roughly equivalent to modern Khurasan. The Parthians fought for the Persians against the victorious Alexander the Great and, when the latter's empire was divided following his death in 323 BC, they came under the governance of Seleucus Nicator. Far from the centre of Seleucid interest, Parthia was governed by a Greek satrap – as was neighbouring Bactria – and like his Bactrian neighbour, the satrap of Parthia took advantage of Seleucid preoccupations in the west to declare independence about the middle of the 3rd century BC. From late in the 4th century BC the area had been invaded by great horsemen of Scythian extraction, prominent among whom, at least at the time of Parthian independence, were the

37 Naqsh-i-Rustam, the humiliation of Valerian by Shapur I Sassanian relief.

An astonishing event, the capture of the Roman emperor was widely proclaimed by the Sassanians and commemorated in rock inscriptions and reliefs at both Naqsh-i-Rustam and Bishapur. The point is made most forcefully by this one carved below the tomb of Darius I – where, of course, it would be seen to revive the glory of the great Achaemenids from whom the Sassanians claimed descent.

Pani. One of their leaders, a chief called Arsaces, presented himself as the deliverer of his kinsmen from the Greeks and seized Parthia from the rebel satrap. Claiming descent from the Achaemenids, his Arsacid dynasty was to last nearly 500 years.

Parthian expansion at Seleucid expense was gradual until the great Mithridates I, who reached the Indus on the one hand and the Tigris on the other. His conquest of Babylonia in 141 BC earned him the title 'King of Kings', though his dynasty's hold on Mesopotamia was consolidated only towards the end of the century under Mithridates II. Further advance westward through Armenia early in the 1st century BC led Parthia into conflict with Rome. In the opening phase the Romans were gravely humiliated by the capture of the Consul Crassus, his legions and their standards at Carrhae in 53. Thereafter fortune switched sides repeatedly in nearly 300 years of confrontation over the Euphrates – despite much internecine rivalry at the Arsacid court – sapping the strength of both powers.

The beneficiary in the east was the Sassanian Ardashir, who claimed descent from the Achaemenids rather more plausibly than Arsaces had done half a millennium earlier. He succeeded in raising a national revolt against the Parthian king, Artabanus V – an able ruler who had recently worsted the Romans. If Ardashir was thus a national hero, his son Shapur I promoted the dynasty to international renown in emulating the Parthian triumph at Carrhae by capturing Valerian. Like the Parthians, too, the Sassanians ruled for over 400 years, their power waxing and waning in conflict with the new Rome of Byzantium but staging a spectacular revival under Chosroes I and II between AD 531 and 628. The end came with the triumph of the Arabs under the Muslim caliph Omar over the last Sassanian king, Yazdegerd III, at Nehavend in 641.

The iwan

The first capital of the Arsacids was at Nisa in Turkmenistan; their last was Ctesiphon, which faced the old Seleucid capital, Seleucia, over the Tigris near modern Baghdad. However, as their monarchy was modelled on that of the Seleucids and centralisation was not strong – at least after Mithridates II, who had no direct heir – there were many important regional centres: the relatively new and prolific former Greek colonies; some still younger ones like Hatra, the seat of Arab desert kings; some of great antiquity like

38 OVERLEAF **Hatra** view of remains with the temple compound in the centre.

Situated between the Tigris and the Euphrates, Hatra's prosperity depended on control of one of the few oases in the northern Mesopotamian desert crossed by the east–west trade route. It was occupied by Arabs in the 1st century BC and was the seat of a monarchy from c. AD 156 to 241. Culturally, at least, it was dependent on both the Romans and the Parthians, though the Romans failed to take it and it remained largely independent of the Parthians. It fell to the Sassanian Shapur I and was then abandoned.

Nearly circular, the city was surrounded by two concentric walls – the outer one of mud brick and nearly 8 kilometres (5 miles) in circumference, the stone inner one punctuated with towers and four gates at the cardinal points. Towards the centre is the great rectangular sanctuary of Shamash, divided into outer and inner wards. In the outer one is a Graeco-Roman temple of uncertain dedication with a recessed fastigium (centre right). Dominating the inner compound (centre background), the main temple and/or palace building consists of two triads of major and minor iwans with an extra two minor ones to the north.

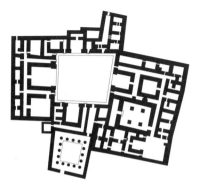

39 **Assur, Parthian palace** early 1st century AD, plan and restored elevation (after the reconstruction in the Pergamon Museum, Berlin).

With its irregular geometry, approximating a central square, this is the earliest-known example of the four-iwan plan – apart, perhaps, from the one at Nisa. If the general approach to planning in terms of a warren of rooms about a nuclear court is traditionally Mesopotamian, like the dominant arch, the eclecticism of the Parthians is marked not only by the Roman dressing, but by the inclusion of a columned hall descended through the Achaemenids from

the Urartians – and, ultimately of course, from the tent. The bands of geometric patterning incised in the gypsum plaster which covered the façade were both classical and native Parthian, perhaps reproducing the patterns of fabric.

The reproduction of the multi-storey palace façade as the scenae frons of the typical Roman theatre, reflected here, did not much precede the reign of Augustus. Of course, this building and the theatrical scenae frons may derive from a common palatial type now best represented by the Library of Celsus at Ephesus or the baths at Sardis (see volume 3, IMPERIAL FORM, pages 228 and 230–31).

Assur, the old Assyrian capital. Leaving the tents of their nomadic past for exposure to the influence of the Hellenised west, in addition to older Persian and Mesopotamian traditions of monumentality, the Parthians and their vassals in these centres evolved a hybrid culture: traditional forms were ordered in the classical manner but without a full understanding of classicism.[38]

The most characteristic feature of Parthian architecture is the great arched iwan, derived through the great arched portals of the Assyrians and Babylonians at least from Mari, but set into a façade reminiscent of a Roman theatrical scenae frons with uncanonical Orders. An early example has been recovered from the ruins at Nisa; a later palace at Assur has four iwans.[39] The Sassanians took up the form for the palaces of their capitals, first for Firozabad in Ardashir's homeland,[40–42] later in the hunting lodge at nearby Sarvistan,[43–44] finally in the imperial capital Ctesiphon.[45]

Behind the iwan, too, Roman influence extended to domed chambers – for the Sassanians, at least – but these were usually cubical in main volume, and the transition from square to circle was effected with arches thrown across the four corners (squinches).

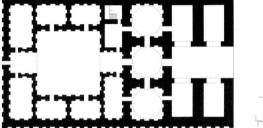

20 m
60 ft

40 **Firozabad, Sassanian palace** plan.

The main façade, facing north, was dominated by the great central iwan (now largely fallen) in which the king could certainly have sat in public audience. Flanked by paired halls for guards and attendants, it led to three great domed rooms well suited to more exclusive reception and private audience. Beyond these was a court flanked by the royal apartments with iwans to the north and south. The traditional tripartite division of the oriental palace has rarely been clearer.

41 Firozabad, Sassanian palace court viewed towards
the north-west with the northern iwan on the right.

42 Firozabad, Sassanian palace central reception room.
   Much of the plaster which presumably once covered the
whole building survives in the domed halls. The eclecticism
of the Sassanians' Achaemenid ancestors is revived in the
decorative detail: note mouldings remotely classical in their
derivation joined to Egyptian coved architraves. Roman
precedents for placing a dome over a square space were
ready to hand: in the baths at Gerasa, for example.

43 **Sarvistan, Sassanian hunting lodge** mid 4th century,
view from the north-west.

In the countryside north-east of Firozabad, this smaller
building – 34 by 42.5 metres (112 by 140 feet) – is generally
dated to the middle of the reign of Shapur II (309–79).
The main domed hall, preceded by an iwan to the north,
was flanked by a court to the east. Both were surrounded by
barrel-vaulted halls, the larger ones to the north and south
with shallow aisles defined by truncated columns – as in a

44 **Sarvistan, Sassanian hunting lodge** detail of dome with oculus and squinches in the main hall.

basilica. The subsidiary domed space in the north-west corner (to the right here) may have been a fire temple: certainly the typical Iranian fire temple is a freestanding domed cube open to all four sides.

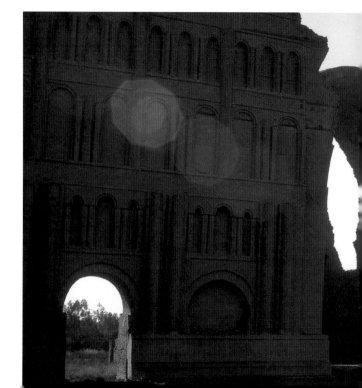

And the domed cube entered the service of Zoroastrianism, revived by the Parthians after the Greek interregnum, as the form of the fire temple.

45 PREVIOUS PAGES **Ctesiphon, Sassanian palace**
mid 6th century, view from the north-east.

Generally attributed to Chosroes I (531–79), this vast brick structure is possibly earlier. As usual with the Sassanians, the palace is oriented with the central iwan facing north. The blind façade to either side of this huge elliptical vault – 24 by 49 metres (80 by 160 feet) rising to 36 metres (120 feet) – screened parallel rows of magazines.

Ctesiphon has taken us far beyond the point where we left Diocletian. Cocooned in a court developing along oriental lines, despite the tetrarchy the elderly emperor remained pre-eminent as dominus in his great camp-palace at Split.[46-47] In 305, however, illness prompted him to resign power, in concert with his associate Maximian, to the assistant Caesars Galerius and Constantius Chlorus. The latter died the following year and, despite the appointment of two new Caesars, his son Constantine was proclaimed emperor. Maximian's son Maxentius challenged this and secured Italy but was finally dispatched by Constantine in 312, at the Milvian Bridge on the northern approach to Rome.[48] Reasserting undivided authority, and ultimately establishing the principle of dynastic succession in place of Diocletian's complex system of power-sharing, Constantine had eliminated the last heirs of the tetrarchy by 323 and promoted the old Greek city of Byzantium to be the imperial capital as Constantinople (now Istanbul) in 330. This second Rome was a world centre for a thousand years.

Diocletian's lasting legacy was an administration concerned primarily with taxation to pay for the army, the bureaucracy and the court. Constantine (324–37)

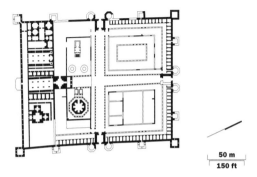

46 Split, Palace of Diocletian c. 300, plan and model.

In its rectangular compound wall – 180 by 212 metres
(592 by 696 feet) – with a gallery overlooking the Adriatic
to the south above a water gate, gates flanked by octagonal
towers to the north, west and east, and square towers at the
corners and towards the middle of each inland section, the
complex was like a great camp. Soldiers and servants seem
to have been lodged in the cells backing on to the walls to
each side of the twin-towered land gates. Each of these

contained square vestibules, presumably always domed, the main one to the north (sometimes called the Golden Gate) providing the emperor with a place of appearance before the world at large. The entrance pavilion to Hadrian's Piazza d'Oro (see 21, page 53) is of the type, while contemporary descriptions suggest that the immediate precedent for both palace and vestibule was provided by the Roman pro-consular palace at Antioch, now vanished, and that this in turn followed a venerable near-eastern tradition descending through the seat of the Hellenistic Seleucids in the same city.

The colonnaded cardo and decumanus crossed in the centre, to the south of accommodation for the household and guests and to the north of the Temple of Jupiter and mausoleum, which were themselves to the north of the main palace buildings. On the central axis, continuing the route from the north which passes between the temple and mausoleum, a portico (fastigium) preceded a domed vestibule, the imperial place of appearance or epiphany. Beyond that an atrium provides the main spine of the private apartments, with various reception rooms balancing one another on either side.

Enshrining the remains of the deified emperor, the mausoleum belongs to the centralised type of building known as a heroum. Diocletian's was octagonal, with alternating rectangular and semi-circular exedrae separated by a ring of columns below a domical vault – like a miniature Pantheon. It provided an immediate precedent for imperial builders of Christian monuments.

47 **Split, Palace of Diocletian** view along peristyle to the fastigium of the main residence with the mausoleum on the left, behind a later tower.

The fastigium, commonly with the architrave curved up into an arch, is at least as plausibly derived from the tent of appearance as from the temple front. The arch, of course, was associated with the place of royal – even divine – appearance from time immemorial. Columns and arches are freely combined in many parts of Diocletian's building, not least to form the gallery overlooking the sea.

reformed the currency and tax system to encourage enterprise and achieved economic revival, but after him the state prospered at the expense of its citizens: many were taxed out of land and industry and their assets passed to the imperial authorities. With state ownership of the means of production, distribution and supply went state organisation of labour – a caste system, tying each worker and his children to a particular job. As any improvement of the individual lot was taxed at a still higher rate, there was little incentive. The vitality and initiative which underlay the prosperity of the old empire were crushed by its successor super-state and stagnation set in. And with stagnation came corruption – not for the last time. Many sought solace in a kingdom that was not of this world.

The popularisation of mystery cults

Rome was tolerant of foreign religions provided they were not seen to be subversive or immoral. In practice, they were licensed under the Law of Association if their adherents were prepared to pay homage to the

48 PREVIOUS PAGES **'Battle of the Milvian Bridge'** fresco by Raphael and his circle (Rome, Vatican Palace).

state gods, particularly to Rome and Augustus, and this was seen as an affirmation of political rather than religious faith. In any case, most pagan cults were concerned with propitiation rites designed to ensure the good will of the gods towards man's achievement of his own will, and these were readily assimilable – indeed the tendency was enshrined in the Pantheon.

Mystery cults had long been popular in Rome: exalting the individual and promising some form of spiritual salvation, they provided the emotional satisfaction wanting in, but not necessarily incompatible with, the state cults. Those of Isis and Serapis were the most important by the time of the destruction of Pompeii in AD 79 and their temples proliferated long after.[49] But there were many others, Hellenic and oriental in origin. By the time of Diocletian those surrounding Mithras and Christ were particularly prominent.

The prestige of Mithras,[50] the Iranian god of light, protector of the righteous and, hence, lord of oaths and guardian of warriors, grew with the de-Romanisation of the army. His cult had been exported to their conquests by the Achaemenids and to the west from Anatolia. Transformed in the process, it came to polyglot

49 **Pergamon, Temple of Serapis** c. 130, south court.

Beyond an extensive cloistered precinct, which bridges the river Selinus, the main hall of the temple was flanked by two smaller colonnaded courts which formed the precincts for a pair of rotundas. The structure was generally of brick clad in marble. A water trough ran down the centre of the main hall's marble pavement to a high podium on which the cult statue stood. This was not directly lit, and a space below the podium penetrated the base of the statue,

50 Mithras slaying the sacred bull 2nd century (Paris, Louvre.)

presumably so that the congregation could be addressed through the god's image.

The stoas of the square side courts were supported by atlantes and caryatids in the ancient Egyptian mode, the male images to one side, the female not exclusively to the other. The paired pools they framed are taken as representing the Nile. It is the Egyptian imagery which has identified the building as a Serapeum, though it is sometimes thought to have been a Mithraeum. It was converted into the basilican church of St John in the early Byzantine period.

Rome with a veneer of Greek anthropomorphic imagery and a veil of mystery borrowed from the initiation rites of Demeter and Bacchus. Sacrificer of the sacred bull, incarnation of primordial existence from whose death came life on earth, Mithras promised eternal life to the initiated – men who had undergone ordeals and performed arcane rites, including sacrificial meals, qualifying them for service as the disciplined champions of the Good. Obviously appealing to soldiers – and the ethos of Rome – the faith expanded rapidly among the legions and reached its apogee, if not with the initiation of Commodus (180–93), then by association with the state cult of Sol Invictus (invincible sun) instituted by Aurelian in 274.

The monotheistic tradition

The followers of Christ were very different – though they too saw themselves as militants and underwent initiation rites qualifying them for service as the champions of the Good. Central to Christ's mystery was his triumph over death, promising rebirth and eternal life to those champions too, and much in his cult was not only paralleled in Mithraism but prefigured in the mysteries of Osiris/Serapis and Isis. But Mithras, Isis and

Serapis – like Rome and Augustus – were prepared to tolerate other gods. The followers of Christ were not. Those other religions admitted of pantheism; Christianity sprang from the resolutely monotheistic tradition of Judaism.

The monotheism of Christ's Jewish ancestors takes primacy for many over all the faiths of antiquity, but it has left no tangible architectural trace beyond the platform of its one great building – the Great Temple of Solomon in Jerusalem, which was finally destroyed by the Romans because of the intransigence of the 'chosen people', loyal only to their One True God. They had been released from Babylonian captivity by the Persians, regrouped and dedicated themselves to sustaining the covenant – the agreement of Moses on Mount Sinai to worship God only and obey his commandments in return for his protection – in beleaguered isolation while awaiting the triumph of their saviour, the second King David: the Messiah. Frustrated under the Seleucids, their anticipation increased in fervour after the Romans annexed Judah with Syria in 63 BC. Ruled through client kings and accorded the privilege of worshipping their God exclusively, their rebelliousness ultimately provoked reprisal and dispersal under Titus in AD 73. Both the privilege and the dispersal favoured the spread of Christianity.

The cult of Jesus

Christianity embraces the mystery of Jesus of Nazareth, a humble descendant of the house of David who began his mission in the second decade of the reign of Tiberius, the third decade of the era that bears his name. He is recorded to have avowed that his mission was to fulfil the word of the prophets, reinstate sacred law and lead man – fallen from grace through his essential freedom of will – back to God. Though apparently careful to distance himself from politics, even to respect Roman authority, he was hailed by his followers as the Messiah come at last – the 'chosen one' ('Christos' in Greek): Son of God. But through the mystery of his birth of the Virgin Mary, he was also seen as the son of man leading a human life on earth: his Father had prepared his human body for sacrifice as a scapegoat in expiation of sin, and promised renewed grace to those with faith in his divine immortality. He was crucified for blasphemy at the instigation of the Jewish hierarchy.[51] And after his sufferings on the cross and death – his Passion – he was indeed seen by his followers as having risen from the dead and ascended into heaven to join his Father. They expected his second coming for the final judgement of man. It was the moral imperative to pass this judgement that distinguished Christianity so sharply from paganism – if not from other mystery religions.

According to the accounts of his mission – the Gospels, written by four of his 12 original disciples – it was the apostle Peter who first recognised Jesus as Christ, and Jesus charged him with the construction of his church. He opened initiation into that church to all through the sacrament of baptism (the cleansing of the soul symbolised by the immersion of the body in water), and sealed the brotherhood of all who would be saved through him in the Eucharist (his sharing of his sacrificed body and blood through the bread and wine of his last supper).

Denounced by the Jewish establishment, however, the church was in fact built abroad, in the world of the gentiles – though, of course, all 12 apostles were Jews joined in the mission by other Jews, most notably Saul of Tarsus who espoused the cause with fervour as Paul and took Christianity to Jews and gentiles in the world at large. And in the world of the gentiles – the world

of Rome – Christianity, as uncompromising in its commitment to the One True God as the Judaism from which it sprang, was bound to clash with imperial paganism. Moreover, though far from unique in their faith in a divine king sacrificed as scapegoat and resurrected as saviour, even in their veneration of a virgin mother – Osiris and Isis come to mind in particular and, indeed, such parallels doubtless assisted in the popularisation of the new faith – Christians set themselves apart with their mysterious rites of initiation and brotherhood and were bound to attract suspicion. But their enemies could only be impressed by their care for one another and their fortitude under persecution.

From persecution to pre-eminence

Persecution of Christians was spasmodic during the first three centuries, though they persistently refused to pay homage to Rome and Augustus. Naturally it was most intense in Rome, where Peter had established his church and the faith was driven underground. Like the pogrom under Nero in 64, persecution was usu-

51 **Studenica, Church of the Virgin, 'Crucifixion of Christ'** sanctuary fresco, c. 1192.

52 Patmos, cave-chapel of St Anne interior.
St John the Divine is reputed to have received his
revelation here. Above, the monastery dedicated to the
saint dates largely from the 11th century.

53 St Simeon Stylites etching.
St Simeon (390–459) is reputed to have spent the last
40 years of his life on top of various columns, the last of
them some 15 metres (49 feet) high.

ally provoked by popular revulsion against a secret society supposedly dedicated to such abominations as eating human flesh and drinking blood – and, misunderstanding notwithstanding, martyrdom is never unwelcome to the zealous. Nor is privation.

Christianity developed in the context of Roman urban life, and during their persecution Christians worshipped in the discretion of their homes or were literally forced underground. Beyond that, after the example of Christ himself and his predecessor, St John the Baptist, the most devout retreated to the wilderness for refuge. Sinai was particularly popular with ascetics because of its remoteness and its venerable association with Moses. St Antony Abbot, who began his particularly inspiring retreat c. 270, came to be seen as the pioneer of Christian monasticism.

Seeking out uncomfortable ways of demonstrating their faith, hermits lodged in caves[52] or even up columns[53] and these were later enshrined. Disciples settled around them. By the middle of the 4th century isolated hermitages of the type inhabited by St Antony were less common than a collection of individual cells loosely associated with one another for communal services. The establishment and ordering of the first such community, in Egypt, is attributed to St Pachomius, who died in 346. Not much later the cells were being linked formally in a compound dominated by a church, a refectory and other communal facilities. Thus the monastery was formed.[54]

Monasticism had reached Syria early in the 4th century and soon spread throughout Mesopotamia. It was taken to the Greek communities of Asia Minor c. 340 and regulated for Greek conditions by St Basil thereafter. Also about 340, it was taken to Rome by St Athanasius and most effectively implanted c. 500 at Monte Cassino in southern Italy by St Benedict (480–544),[55] who was the first to institute a non-arbitrary rule of monastic life adapted to the conditions of the west. But that is to look ahead.

54 OVERLEAF **Sinai, St Catherine's monastery**
6th century and later.

The fortress enclosing a church, monastery and barracks was built by the Emperor Justinian as part of the outer defences of Palestine. Most of the buildings inside stand in place of the originals, but the church (c. 540) retains much of the original fabric including the timber roof and some of the finest mosaics of the pre-iconoclastic period.

Cum domibus istis pluribus parata accipe libros.

Rupta lectus presto. Cely michi possiancy esto.

Towards the end of the 3rd century general measures were taken against a perceived threat to the imperial state from an expanding, well-organised force which refused army service but fervently sought the second coming of its Messiah and the destruction of all except the faithful – including, of course, the Roman empire. The mandatory performance of sacrifice by all citizens, certified by a magistrate, and the punishment of those refusing to comply, especially harsh for imperial officials admitting Christian sympathies, had not proved enough. Diocletian and Galerius took the final steps in 303: all Christians were deprived of Roman citizenship and with it the right to hold office and the full protection of the law; priests were to be imprisoned and forced to sacrifice; churches were to be destroyed wholesale. Yet citizenship meant little more than tax liability to many, while the church offered communion of a very different kind. Where the magistrate represented oppression, the bishop promised salvation.

Only eight years later Galerius issued the Edict of

55 St Benedict and the foundation of Monte Cassino
manuscript illustration.

Toleration, the persistence of great numbers in the Christian faith was admitted, the measures against them were withdrawn and they were required to pray for public welfare. Hardly two years more and Constantine reputedly acknowledged that his victory over Maxentius had been achieved under the sign of the cross of Jesus Christ, who thus charged him with his mission to preserve and prosper the empire. Though he confessed the faith exclusively only on his deathbed in 337, through Constantine the divine Augustus had become vice-regent for Christ.

Denying the competence of the state to interfere in matters of conscience, indeed sustaining Rome's old tradition of religious tolerance, Constantine and his successors fostered a *catholic* church in the belief that Christian unity was the key to imperial unity. After Julian the Apostate's quixotic attempt to restore the old gods in 361, Theodosius I finally withdrew tolerance in 378 – but now paganism was proscribed and the temples expropriated.

Consolidation of doctrine

With no scripture left by Christ himself but four different accounts of his mission and sayings, the early Christian movement was plagued by doctrinal difference. Official recognition and the imperial will to reinforce political unity with a church catholic in practice – as the faith was catholic in principle – promoted the definition of canonical dogma from the Gospels and the epistles of the apostles to the early churches. For this purpose the first of a series of general councils was convened at the emperor's behest in his palace at Nicaea in 325. It defined the concept of the Trinity – central to the faith in God the Father, Son and Holy Ghost – in terms of God one in substance but three in persons, and hence determined the creed to be affirmed by all the faithful.

This orthodoxy was not to go unchallenged, but in the quest for resolution the church acquired intellectual standing to rival the pagan philosophers through the contributions of great theologians. Among those writing before the end of the 4th century were Ambrose, who defended the eternity of Christ's godhead against the so-called Arian heresy that he was created by, and therefore must be in some measure inferior to, the Father; Jerome, who undertook the task of producing a canonical Latin text of the Bible in the 380s; and Augustine, who, observing the fall of

Rome from a distance, contrasted the vitality of Christianity with the mortality of paganism in terms of two cities, temporal and spiritual, in his great treatise *The City of God*.

The fall of Rome

Imperial unity was based on a common language, coinage and law, an international army and long-established patterns of trade. But a primarily non-Roman army was inherently unreliable and economic development, not least as a result of Constantine's reforms, laid the foundations for provincial self-sufficiency. With their old urban civilisation and prominent merchant class, Egypt and Syria were increasingly difficult to contain. In the less-developed west, on the other hand, long prey to unsettled and unsettling barbarian forces, the old aristocracy entrenched itself and consolidated its estates as power bases independent of – even hostile to – the crumbling imperial regime.

Having reversed Diocletian's religious policy, Theodosius I revived his predecessor's state policy: in 393 he divided the succession between his two sons, Rome and the provinces west of Italy passing to Honorius and Constantinople and the eastern provinces to

56 Constantinople (Istanbul), defensive wall
constructed between 408 and 413, western range.

The ramparts here provide the earliest significant surviving example of a double ring of walls within a moat for defence in depth – though the principle was known to the ancient Indians among others. The main wall, punctuated by 96 rectangular towers, was 7 kilometres (4.5 miles) in extent, 9 metres (30 feet) high and 5 metres (16 feet) thick. It was built of concrete reinforced with courses of brick and faced with limestone blocks.

Arcadius. Neither proved competent. Arcadius (395–408) and his successors defended Constantinople,[56] but Honorius (393–423) lost Rome. From the middle of the 4th century the pressure of barbarian hordes on Rome had led to the removal of the imperial seat to northern provincial centres: first Milan, then Ravenna where Honorius went in 410 to escape Alaric the Visigoth. Under his sister Galla Placidia, regent for her son Valentinian III (425–55), and their ephemeral successors, Ravenna remained the capital until the western empire's end.

After sacking Rome in 410, the Visigoths took Provence and Spain. Much of central and northern France had fallen to the Franks by 460. Meanwhile the Vandals, who had taken north Africa, crossed the sea to sack Rome in 455. In 476, finally, the last western emperor, Romulus Augustulus, abdicated under pressure from the Herulean Ostrogoths. Embracing the Arian creed, like most of the western barbarians on their conversion to Christianity, the Ostrogoths occupied much of north-eastern Italy and provided a period of relative stability from 495 to 526 under their king Theodoric – who maintained Ravenna as his capital.[57]

In the absence of an imperial establishment in the west, the church was the sole authority of supranational significance, especially with the conversion of hordes of the barbarians who had destroyed the empire. An early hierarchy of government within the church derived from the office of the apostles but developed in parallel to the secular administration, with bishoprics grouped into provinces presided over by archbishops or metropolitans. Despite the significance of the then imperial capital and the prestige of Peter, primacy does not seem to have been accorded to the Bishop of Rome in the first Christian centuries, though recognition of the need for strong central government in the church preceded the abdication of Romulus Augustulus. Pope Leo I, who died 15 years earlier, asserted the primacy of his office – and even the Arian Vandals, Visigoths and Ostrogoths were prepared to concede this – but it was more than a century until Pope Gregory I (590–604) formally assumed the care of all the churches. Consolidation of papal power proceeded over another 500 years at least, to its culmination in face of a revival of the emperor's title.

Church and state in the east

In the east the survival of the emperor as constituted authority had the opposite effect in inhibiting centralisation of power in the church. As the 'Thirteenth Apostle' and chairman of the supreme ecclesiastical synod, the emperor appointed the heads of the several national churches of the imperial domain and was

57 Ravenna, S Apollinare Nuovo, mosaic of a Byzantine imperial palace.

The canonical basilican church was dedicated in 490 by the Ostrogothic king Theodoric to St Martin.

Usually identified as Theodoric's palace, references have not surprisingly been detected in the image here both to the Palace of Diocletian at Split (see 46, pages 110–11) and to the imperial palace at Constantinople (see 58, pages 146–47). The twin-towered portal (right), symbol of royal power from time immemorial, could derive from either the Golden Gate of the former or the main entrance (Chalka) of the latter. The fastigium, flanked by the colonnades of a peristyle, clearly recalls Diocletian's (see 47, page 113) – though the colonnades at Split are at right angles to it. Note the galleried upper storey, not present in the peristyle at Split, but known to Constantine's builders.

pleased to see them as largely autonomous and equal in jurisdiction, if not quite in honour, to the Patriarch of Constantinople. And the number of these churches increased as the Slavic tribes, who had penetrated eastern Europe in the wake of the hordes which sapped Rome, were converted to Christianity by missionaries from the east. But the differences between the eastern and western churches were not merely of structure: post-Nicene doctrinal disputes (in particular over the west's contention that the Holy Ghost descended from the Father and the Son), divergence in the process of the Eucharist and denial of the primacy of the pope were among the main causes of the Great Schism effected in 1054, the east claiming that it alone was orthodox.

Doctrinal difference, mainly over the nature of Christ – whether he was wholly divine or part-human – also divided the provinces of the east. In brief, the Egyptian church of Alexandria maintained that the human and the divine were united indistinguishably in him (monophysitism). Syrian Antioch maintained that they co-existed separately. Constantinople reached accord with Rome in 451 in embracing two natures, perfect and perfectly distinct (dyophysitism). Egypt and Syria rejected this, and their monophysitism bolstered their separatism, based on the prosperity of their individual economies.

Under strong emperors like Justinian (527–65), Constantinople was the capital of a revived empire whose arms recovered much of Italy, north Africa and even southern Spain. However, reforms at the centre, promoted by imperial ministers who were seen as oppressive, nearly led to disaster: in 532 the factions into which the city's population was divided for competition in the hippodrome – but which acquired distinct political complexions from their identification with specific classes – found themselves exceptionally at one in insurrection (the Nike riots). In the face of the destruction of most of the capital, the emperor was on the verge of flight, but his remarkable empress Theodora stiffened his resolve. He survived, continued the reforms – not the least of which was the codification of the whole corpus of Roman law since Hadrian – and rebuilt the capital with exceptional magnificence.[58]

The renovated institutions bequeathed by Justinian stood the empire in good stead for centuries. And the reform process continued: Maurice (582–602) reor-

58 OVERLEAF **Constantinople** plan of central area
as rebuilt under Justinian from 532 (according to a
reconstruction of 1906 based primarily on documentary
evidence).

(1) Hagia Sophia north of (2) the Augustaeum (the main
public forum), with west (3) the Milion, the baldacchino-
like ceremonial tetrapylon through which the emperor
entered or left the imperial quarters of his capital, east (4)
the senate, and south (5) the Chalka, the main ceremonial
entrance vestibule to the great palace which culminates in
(6) the throne room, Chrysotriclinos. To the west are (7) the
Baths of Zeuxippus and (8) the hippodrome. At the far left
(9) is Hagia Eirene, at the far right (10) SS Sergius and
Bacchus.

Byzantium was founded in the 7th century BC as a
Dorian colony. Much developed in the early 3rd century AD
under the Emperor Septimius Severus, it was chosen by
Constantine as his new capital because of its strategic
position in relationship to the rich provinces of the eastern
parts of the empire, its relative remoteness from barbarian
threat, its harbour and its defensible narrow isthmus.

Little survives from Constantine's period, indeed virtually
nothing of secular importance remains from the so-called
Byzantine period at all – other than the magnificent walls

(see 56, page 137) and the spectacular forest of columns rising from the underground water cisterns (now known as Yerebatan Saray). One of the main squares of the modern city is formed by the perimeter of the hippodrome – the main arena for public entertainment in the new capital, which was originally built by Septimius Severus c. 200, enlarged by Theodosius I in the 380s and then embellished with a fragment of an Egyptian obelisk on a base still surviving on site.

The great palace to its south-east – its terraced courts and pavilions many times extended, renovated and rebuilt over the long course of Byzantine history – is imaginatively reconstructed here in its 6th-century state along the formal lines of the Domus Augustana on the Roman Palatine (see 10, page 29). All has disappeared under the 17th-century mosque of Ahmed Shah and its precincts. Descriptions of court ritual and the history of Justinian's reign written by Procopius make it clear that the Chalka (the House of Bronze because of its doors) was the first of many domed vestibules to successive parts of the palace, each a canopy-like pavilion for the epiphany ritual of an emperor who, as vicar of Christ, equal to the apostles, retained a measure of the religious significance of his pagan predecessors. Sustaining a long tradition embracing the entrance pavilion

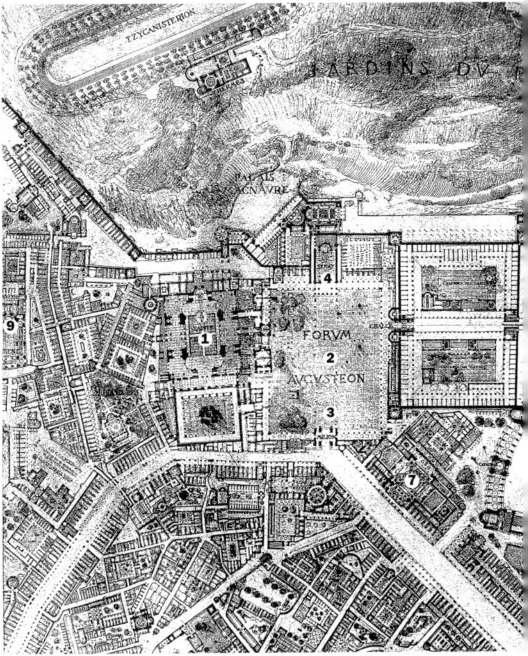

TZYCANISTERION

IARDINS DV

PALAIS
MAGNAVRE

9

1

4

FORVM
2
AVGVSTEON

3

7

of Hadrian's Piazza d'Oro at Tivoli (see 20, page 52) – if not the
tri-lobed triclinium there (see 17, page 48) – and the vestibule of
the Palace of Diocletian at Split (see 46, page 110), the Chalka
was originally built by Constantine between towers in the
ramparts of his citadel. Probably domed from the outset,
like Diocletian's work, according to Procopius it was rebuilt
by Justinian as a cruciform hall, the main axis running
north–south, with a central dome and vaulted arms.
Contemporary references suggest that there was a chapel
on an upper level and a gallery or balcony of appearance
between the towers. As in Hadrian's Villa, the scene of
ultimate epiphany was the throne room, here restored as
a quatralobe, though others see it as tri-lobed or octagonal.

Domestic architecture in Byzantium seems rarely to have
matched the scale or standards of old Rome. To the north
of the hippodrome, however, excavation since 1906 has
revealed the remains of a noble palace dating from the
early 5th century. The main elements are two semi-circular
courts, their axes roughly at right angles to one another, the
smaller one with a rotunda at its head, the larger one with
a boldly niched hexagon flanked by rotundas and octagons.
The relationship of the main room, circular or hexagonal,
to an open exedra recalls the representational core of Nero's
Domus Aurea (see 13, page 38).

ganised the provincial administration into exarchies[59] (such as Italy and Africa) divided into duchies. But Maurice and his heirs fell to the mutiny of their unpaid soldiers. The ensuing strife was terminated by Heraclius (610–41) who paid the soldiers by settling them on lands confiscated from dissident nobles: they formed *themes* identified with their former regiments, and these became units of local administration which, like Maurice's duchies, marked the political map for centuries to come.

Heraclius went on to military victory throughout the empire, not least against Persia after the assassination of the Sassaninan king Chosroes II in 628. But he had no more success than his predecessors in solving the problems of doctrinal difference. Disaffected Egypt and Syria were ready prey to the Arab forces unleashed following the death of the Prophet Muhammad in 632 and the advent of Islam. Mesopotamia was lost before the decade was out; Alexandria fell in 642; and the whole of north Africa was soon to follow.

There was periodic revival under effective rulers, but the rump of the empire was prey to stultifying bureaucracy, expanded with conquest but not con-

59 Ravenna, so-called Palace of the Exarch late
6th/7th century.

The composition, with superimposed arches between
massive bays, probably reflects the form of the Chalka at

tracted in defeat, and undermined by internal religious conflict allied to ethnic differences. This ultimately proved disastrous in the face of vigorous external pressure. Yet cultural prestige and skilful diplomacy – based on readiness to compromise with the barbarians if they acknowledged the emperor and Christianity – sustained Constantinople for nearly a millennium after the empire had reached its peak.

Italy was finally lost to the Lombards in the middle of the 8th century and soon disintegrated into independent duchies. Venice, one of several island settlements of refugees from the barbarians, had been incorporated into the empire under Justinian and ruled by a duke nominated by the emperor. It asserted its independence in the 9th century. By the 11th century, on the strength of trade and a prominent role in transporting and provisioning the crusaders sent at several reprises to recover the Holy Land from the Muslims, it had an empire along the shores of the Adriatic and

Constantinople (see 58, pages 144–45). Blind at the top, open below, the side bays recall the piers of the triumphal arch, which itself has been recognised as a formal derivative from the ancient Mesopotamian twin-towered portal of epiphany.

special trading privileges throughout the remains of the empire.

By 1202 the Venetians were powerful – and shameless – enough to deflect the Fourth Crusade to the sack of Constantinople and the virtual termination of the Byzantine empire two years later. By then, in fact, Byzantium had been reduced to Greece by the Slavs and Bulgars in the Balkans and the Seljuk Turks in Asia Minor. The Ottoman Turks, who had embraced Islam and filled the power vacuum left by the Mongol destruction of the Seljuks at the beginning of the 14th century, delivered the final blow and occupied Constantinople on 29 May 1453.

East and west, Christianity promoted a new kind of art and architecture, anti-classical – non-humanist – in essence. In the main, Christians rejected the celebration of this world, in particular the idealisation of man as reflecting the image of god. Denying that the divine could be deduced from the observation of physical phenomena and expressed in the rational terms of pure geometry or mathematical proportions, it deposed the mind of man from the central position humanism had assigned it as the controlling force to which everything is comprehensible. On the contrary, Christianity and its art saw this world as merely a base prelude to the glory to come, a glory that is not susceptible to reason but attainable only through faith in the operation of a transcendental power incarnate as Christ.

Look at the frieze from the Athenian Parthenon (see volume 2, HELLENIC CLASSICISM, page 124) or the frescoes from the Villa of the Mysteries in Pompeii (see volume 3, IMPERIAL FORM, page 170) and compare them with a Byzantine image of the crucified Christ (see 51, page 124). In the Parthenon frieze, the sculptor Phidias offers a supreme statement of the will to idealise and to represent that ideal realistically in space: the relief is shallow, but the figures and horses appear to stand naturally one in front of the other. The Pompeian artist may not be as great, but he realises a similar objective under the even tougher constraint of working in only two dimensions. In both cases the foreshortening of form depends on the rational analysis of the principles of perspective and the perceived diminution of objects in space. The Byzantine artist, by contrast, has not been interested in constructing images of corporeality or tangible space for his figures – let alone the cross – to stand on. They are like cardboard cut-outs superimposed against a flat background in which the reality of perspective has not been forgotten but ignored as irrelevant.

The Christian artist is concerned with the super-natural, with God as man not man as god, and with an other-worldly hierarchy: his images are icons, timeless ideograms abstracted from physical reality whose spiritual significance eclipses that reality. The classical artist conveys an ideal of physical beauty worthy of the gods. The Christian artist conveys the spiritual ideals of God's sacrificial mystery, of suffering, of compassion, of devotion – and of motherhood.

Representation versus iconoclasm

Yet, of course, a measure of classical anthropomorphism survived even in this. Indeed, there was a school of Christian thought, identified as neo-Platonic, which maintained that through the contemplation of that which could be seen the mind might rise to comprehend that which could not be seen. From the idea that the seen suggests the unseen it was a short step to the belief that the seen *contains* the unseen.

Christian purists had long opposed anthropomorphism as contravening the second commandment passed from God to Moses on Mount Sinai (thou shalt not make to thyself any graven image, nor the likeness of any thing that is in heaven above...) and at first Christ was represented only through symbols such as the cross or the lamb of the good shepherd's protection and of the sacrifice. The purists, however, were contradicted with the contention that as God had assumed human form in Christ, he should be so represented. The orderer of creation, moreover, his order could be reflected in the pure geometry of the church – the image of his heavenly mansion. The realisation of an ideal order in the geometry of the church was an eastern achievement after the 6th century, as we shall see. Growth in popular veneration of icons was dramatic after the 5th century, when the earliest-known image of the Crucifixion appeared. In reaction, Emperor Leo III issued a decree proscribing them in 730. The wholesale destruction of images throughout the Byzantine world resulted. The proscription was lifted by the Council of Nicaea in 787 but iconoclasm persisted until 843.

The origins of the church

The principal object of Christian architecture was, of course, the church. But as Christians entered the fold through baptism and had often left it through martyrdom, special buildings (the baptistry and martyrium) were required to provide for the one and commemorate the other. Christians were interred like most other Romans, usually in subterranean warrens (catacombs). And among the earliest of Christian buildings were great halls providing for the obsequial rites at burial sites.

The origin of the church was in the house: [60] Christianity developed in the context of Roman urban life and during their persecution Christians worshipped in the discretion of their homes. When they emerged from

60 **Qirqbize, house church** 5th century, entrance.

persecution and were able to build churches openly they rejected the temple as a model, for both pragmatic and symbolic reasons. The beliefs enshrined in the temple were, of course, anathema, but the Christians also rejected the form because it was non-congregational.

Christianity was a proselytising religion in need of large congregational spaces in which the Gospel could be preached and the mystery of the Eucharist revealed. The typical basilica, with its nave for seating and its aisles for access, provided just such a space, but the Christians also favoured it for its symbolic significance. Certainly not invariably, but most usually, the basilica was an elongated hall of judgement in which the magistrate dominated the assembly from his throne on the dais in the apse at the end. Appropriating the form in its triumph, Christianity substituted the infallible judgement of God for the fallible judgement of man – and the bishop as Christ's vicar for the magistrate as the representative of secular power.

There were simple Christian basilicas before Constantine, but after him the church was an official body closely linked to the imperial administration and it became increasingly hierarchical. Led by bishops of imperial rank, the clergy separated itself from the laity and naturally it found the common house unpropitious – indeed, the emperor made the point himself and called for a building type of the highest dignity and materials of the greatest richness. Codified under imperial auspices, the liturgy of service to the Lord, represented by the bishop, followed the ritual of the emperor's court, including processions preceded by insignia to the episcopal throne and altar.[61] These were given baldacchinos like the imperial throne and, of course, the imperial throne was displayed in the principal room of the palace, a magisterial basilica. ('Basilica', indeed, derives from the Greek for 'place of the king'.) Palace imagery thus pervaded the Christian conception of the church – as both a building apart and the institution of God's elect and, beyond all, of God's heavenly mansion to which the church was the door (see 57, page 140).

The intermixture of religious and secular imagery is crucial in the conception of both the palace and the church, and though the Christians rejected classical humanism their architecture derived from the building types of the Romans. The triumphal arch has been seen as the classical descendent of the twin-towered gate of the ancient Mesopotamian palace. Both were

places of epiphany, of the appearance of god among men, the triumphal arch commemorating the progress of state hero or emperor from mortality to immortality: apotheosis. As such its symbolism is of obvious relevance to a faith centred on the concept of resurrection, and the form was adopted for the portal of the church. It was certainly also remembered for the palace of the Christian emperor – or his representative, the exarch (see 59, page 150).

If the church was distinct from other buildings, within it distinct spaces, hierarchically ordered, accommodated different functions. The primary distinction, of course, was of the sanctuary from the place of lay congregation, but separate provision also had to be made for catechumens and for their baptism. Baptism was originally administered by total immersion and the buildings accommodating it were naturally focused on the central event of the sacrament.[62]

61 **Rome, S Agnese** 625, apse and throne.
A necropolis pilgrimage church, S Agnese was built into the burial mound so that direct access from outside to galleries overlooking the nave and the saint's tomb relieved pressure on that main level.

The centralised form, often polygonal but nevertheless generated as a circle from a single centre, derived from the Greek tholos. It was also the natural form of the heroum or tomb, ideally focused on the monument or grave of the incumbent, and the early Christians adopted it to enshrine the spot where saints were martyred or buried.

The works of Constantine

Constantine founded the pre-eminent basilicas of Christendom as the cathedral of Rome, S Giovanni in Laterano, beside the palace he gave to the Bishop of Rome soon after the Battle of the Milvian Bridge, and over the grave of St Peter, to whom Christ had entrusted the keys of his church. From the house his architects extracted the atrium and expanded it into a forecourt. From the variety of basilican forms produced over nearly half a millennium they chose the longitudinal plan with colonnaded aisles for communication to each side of a wider, higher nave terminating in a raised apse and lit through windows in its

62 **Ravenna, Arian baptistry** c. 500, vault with mosaic showing the baptism of Christ.

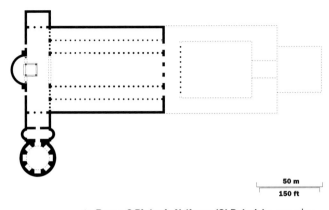

63 **Rome, S Pietro in Vaticano (St Peter's)** c. 330, plan.

Designed as a cemetery church intended for obsequial rites rather than for the regular celebration of mass before a permanent congregation, this formidable basilica – 64 metres (210 feet) wide and 112 metres (368 feet) long from door to apse – was begun after Constantine had left for his new capital and its construction seems to have dragged on at least until 390. Preceded by a cloistered atrium, the main building had a broad central nave – 84 by 58 metres (276 by 196 feet) – flanked by double aisles.

Work started at the west end, where the 2nd-century
monument reputedly enshrining the apostle's tomb was
embraced by a cross-arm inserted between nave and apse
– the first important transept in Christian architecture. The
mausoleum of the Emperor Honorius was later attached
to the transept's south arm. Last to be completed to the
original plan was the atrium which provided for entry from
the east – unusually, as the tradition was yet to be firmly
established that Christian churches were built so that the
priest at the altar faced east (hence the word orientation).

The basilica was built of splendid materials. Placed
impressively close together – at centres of 2.5 metres
(8 feet) – the columns were pillaged from earlier buildings
and widely varied in stone texture and colour. The capitals
were oddly assorted Corinthian and Composite of different
heights. Above them, between 11 windows to each side,
the clerestory – rising to 37 metres (120 feet) – was frescoed
in the 5th century with scenes from the Old Testament.
Over the tomb a ciborium was carried on spiral columns.
Still preserved in the great 16th-century building which
replaced Constantine's work, these are supposed to have
come from – or at least emulated – the Great Temple of
Solomon in Jerusalem and their form is consequently
known as Solomonic.

64 **Rome, S Pietro in Vaticano** fresco by Raphael,
'Fire in the Borgo' (Rome, Vatican Palace).

The characteristic Christian basilican profile of high
nave flanked by low aisles is clearly recorded here in rich
chromaticism which was not characteristic of the façades
of Constantine's period – as in the great buildings of the
imperial past, decorative splendour was internal.

upper walls (clerestory) and roofed in timber. In
S Pietro in Vaticano (St Peter's),[63–64] embracing the
earlier tomb of the apostle, a lateral hall was interpolated in front of the apse to provide extra space for pilgrims and the symbolism of the cross. Separating
sanctuary from nave, this transept admirably served
the official church's hierarchical purpose and was to
be usual practice throughout the history of Christian
architecture – at least in the west.

The earliest baptistries had usually been square –
even rectangular – but beside the Lateran basilica Constantine's architects seem to have initiated the singu-
larly appropriate octagonal plan.[65] Only parts of the
outer walls have survived subsequent refurbishment,
but the idea of a colonnade screening an ambulatory
from the font was probably original – it is merely an
adaptation to a centralised form of the standard procedure for screening nave from aisles in a rectangular
basilica.

The motif reappears on a grander scale in the mausoleum of the emperor's daughter Constantina, now
known as S Costanza.[66] Built beside the covered cemetery of S Agnese, this is the most complete surviving
example of the typical early Christian centralised

shrine. The focal point of such a building, naturally in the centre, was the obvious site for the tomb (or font) and the axis of entry, established at no one point on the essentially uniform circumference, had arbitrarily to be extended for the altar. Here, in fact, an altar occupies the centre and the sarcophagus is sheltered by a recession in the ambulatory opposite the entrance.

Constantine's architects were experimental and certainly did not confine themselves to standard types. They were responsible for developing and combining centralised and longitudinal forms in works now known largely only from descriptions. In Constantinople the Church of the Holy Apostles, built as his mausoleum, was cruciform with a central dome sheltering the emperor's sarcophagus and statues of the 12 apostles – with whom he was to be venerated on equal terms. At Antioch, the imperial palatine chapel was octagonal with semi-circular

65 **Rome, baptistry of S Giovanni in Laterano** c. 330, c. 430 and later, interior.

The present arrangement of superimposed Orders descends from the remodelling carried out on the instructions of Pope Sixtus III (432–40). Ceilings are later.

66 **Rome, S Costanza** c. 350, interior.

A barrel-vaulted ambulatory is screened from the domed
rotunda housing the altar by a colonnade in the way that
the rectangular nave was screened from the aisles in a
basilica. Uncanonically, however, the columns carry arches
rather than a flat entablature.

exedrae to the sides and an ambulatory over which a second level of colonnades provided a gallery. Galleries were not new: the form is implicit in the upper colonnade of the typical Greek temple interior and reappears in works like the Pompeian basilica. Constantine's architects further adopted it in the complex enshrining the place of Christ's crucifixion and the Church of the Holy Sepulchre in Jerusalem[67] which, like the Church of the Nativity at Bethlehem, combined the basilica with the martyrium.

Standardisation and variation

After Constantine there was a period in which types were clarified, forms consolidated, details regulated. A standard was set in the many new basilicas built in and around Rome to commemorate the most important early Christians associated with the growth of the church in the then imperial capital.[68] Moreover, after the vigorous, if somewhat indiscriminate, re-use of materials pillaged from temples under Constantine and his immediate successors, there was a relatively brief and selective revival of classical order in the later 4th century, in concert with the consolidation of form in planning. The finest marble for new work

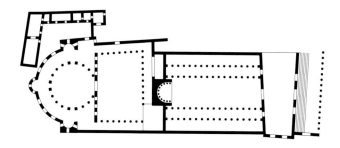

20 m
60 ft

67 Jerusalem, Church of the Holy Sepulchre on Golgotha c. 328–36, plan.

According to his chroniclers, Constantine ordered a church more beautiful than any other to be built on the site of Christ's Passion. Here, the tomb traditionally identified as the one from which Christ rose from the dead seems to have been cut from its cliff, and the ground to the east levelled around and beyond the rock of Calvary – site of the

crucifixion – which was also cut to shape. Little of
Constantine's work survives later rebuilding – especially
by the Crusaders in the 12th century – but according to
a contemporary description (by Constantine's historian
Eusebius), both the sacred places were embraced by a
cloistered precinct, and a tempietto of 12 columns, the
Anastasis, was erected as a ciborium for the tomb.
A double-aisled basilica, with galleries over the aisles
perhaps for the first time in a major Christian building,
and its atrium entered through a propylaeum were built
over the eastern half of the site, butting on to the ancient
street giving access to it. The semi-circle of the usual apse
was continued round the ends of the flanking sacristies to
form three-quarters of a rotunda. Twelve columns, one
for each apostle, ringed its interior in resonance with the
tempietto over the tomb: the precise form of this element
remains undetermined but it may have been destined for
the true cross rediscovered by the emperor's mother, the
Empress Dowager Helena.

   The Church of the Nativity at Bethlehem, c. 333 but
also rebuilt or renovated several times, seems to have
included a cloistered atrium, a double-aisled basilica and
an octagonal shrine sheltering the cave in which Christ is
believed to have been born.

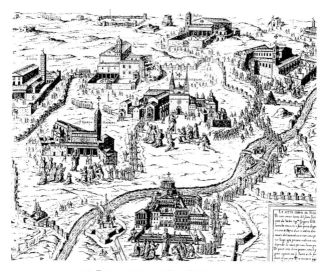

68 Rome, seven major pilgrimage churches late
16th-century engraving showing S Giovanni in Laterano
(centre), S Pietro in Vaticano (bottom), then (clockwise)
S Maria Maggiore, S Lorenzo fuori le Mura, S Croce in
Gerusalemme, S Sebastiano, S Paolo fuori le Mura.

At the instigation of the Empress Dowager Helena, a hall of her palace perhaps was converted into the basilican S Croce to enshrine a relic of the cross on which Christ was crucified. S Lorenzo on the Via Tiburtina and S Sebastiano on the Via Appia originated under Constantine as basilican halls built over the cemeteries where the saints were buried. Set into the terraced site of the cemetery, S Lorenzo was rebuilt from 579 with galleries over the aisles, like S Agnese, to provide upper-level access to relieve the pressure of pilgrims on the main floor: galleries, familiar in the east after the construction of the Church of the Holy Sepulchre in Jerusalem, had not hitherto been common in Rome. As in S Sebastiano, the aisles continued around the apsidal end wall to form an ambulatory for the circulation of the pilgrims. The lavish basilica of S Paolo, on the Via Ostiense burial site previously enshrined by Constantine, was built from 385 to accommodate the apostle in a way comparable with that of St Peter. Double-aisled, with carefully matched columns and newly carved capitals carrying arches perhaps for the first time on this scale, the nave was 97 metres (318 feet) long and 24 metres (79 feet) wide; a transept embraced the tomb, as at S Pietro in Vaticano, but it hardly projected beyond the main body of the building. S Paolo was rebuilt after a disastrous fire in 1823.

came from the imperial quarries on the island of Proconnesos in the Sea of Marmara.

Classical order is well represented in S Maria Maggiore,[69] but only slightly earlier at S Paolo fuori le Mura, as later in Ravenna (see 57, page 140), arches continued to spring from columns, routinely rather than with symbolic significance. The new capitals of S Paolo were canonical, but impost blocks were added early in the 5th century to accommodate uncanonical arches and mouldings which in general strayed from the classical norm. In Ravenna, as in Constantinople, the Corinthian acanthus became a gauze of intricately chiselled and undercut stylised foliage, often with figurative elements superimposed. It retained its identity

A standard basilican plan, approximated in these varied works, was fixed in their smaller contemporaries, such as S Clemente (built c. 380 over the city's main Mithraeum). Beyond an atrium, a broad, short nave terminating in a semi-circular apse but no transept was flanked by two aisles continuing around the west end to form a putative exonarthex. S Sabina (c. 422) achieved the canonical in adjusting the proportions of the nave with greater height and length.

69 **Rome, S Maria Maggiore** 432–40, nave.

The classical basilica with one aisle to each side of
a nave screened by a consistent Order of columns is
well represented by S Maria Maggiore. The conception
responded to the regularising incentive of a classical
revival under Pope Sixtus III inspired specifically by the
Basilica of Trajan. Some of the mosaic panels above the
near-canonical Ionic Order are original but the ciborium
and ceiling are later.

70 **Qalbloze, parish church** late 5th century, interior.
The basilican plan is sustained in primitive purity,
without transepts, but colonnades give way to arcades
springing low from truncated piers, and the classicism of
the detail is wayward, in the manner of nearby Qalat-Siman
(see 78, pages 190–91).

71 **Cairo, S Sergius** late 5th century, much renovated, interior.

The church was built on a site associated with the holy family's flight into Egypt. The single-aisled basilica was rebuilt in the 12th century and an iconostasis was interpolated. The decoration is post-Islamic.

longer elsewhere but was often windswept into asymmetry in Syria in particular.

The basilica, usually with one aisle to each side, was the norm for the congregational church, large and small, throughout Christendom. However, just as the ancient Roman basilica was varied in form, so too the shape of its early Christian successor was dictated by many considerations which took precedence over respect for a remote metropolitan model.[70-71] In accordance with liturgical developments and regional traditions, new elements were added to the standard formula. Transepts were integrated with the main body by extending the aisle arcades into them or partitioned in subordination by extending the arcades across them.[72] The latter method tended to distinguish the central crossing, before the apse, in furtherance of liturgical purpose as it developed in the 5th century, especially in the east.

In the west the congregation remained in the nave, but in the east the clergy claimed the nave as well as the sanctuary: the latter for the celebration of the Eucharist, the manifestation of the flesh of God, the former for readings from the scripture and preaching, the manifestation of the word of God. The sanctuary

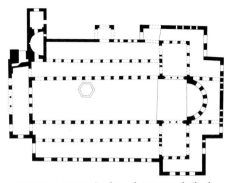

72 **Salonica, S Demetrius** late 5th century, rebuilt after
a fire in 1917, plan.

The double-aisled basilica with transepts subsists, but
the outer aisle continues around the transepts and apse.
Galleries over the inner aisle continue over the narthex.
Piers punctuate the nave colonnades to produce a rhythm
of 4:5:4 bays over which the columns carry arches on both
levels. The line of the nave colonnade is continued by
a smaller Order, screening the chancel from the transept
arms in assertion of its distinction. The lines of the nave
colonnades continue beyond the apse to screen the central
section of the ambulatory.

was closed to the sight of the laity and even the nave was screened from them as they were restricted to the aisles, narthex and atrium. To relieve the consequent pressure on congregational space, the aisles were sometimes surmounted by galleries and/or extended across the end of the nave to double the narthex (ex-onarthex). Towers appear to either side of the portal, perhaps first in Syria where the propylaea of temples had long sustained the ancient Mesopotamian tradition of the twin-towered gate as the place of epiphany.

Martyrium and baptistry were now usually polygonal or circular: the attempt to expand the form to provide for a parish congregation in S Stefano Rotondo[73] was apparently deemed unsuccessful – at least in the west. As at Antioch, however, centralised forms derived from the place of the emperor's appearance in

73 Rome, S Stefano Rotondo first half of the 5th century, interior.

Probably to enshrine a relic of the earliest of early Christian martyrs, the architect of this impressive work recalled the form of S Costanza (see 66, page 170) and elaborated it. The main centralised space is ringed by an Ionic colonnade forming an ambulatory which cedes

nothing in its regularity to the colonnaded aisles of S Maria
Maggiore (see 69, page 177). The tall clerestory is part of
the original conception but not the present vault. Beyond
the ambulatory the spatial arrangement has been changed.
A further colonnade seems to have screened alternating
chapels and semi-circular courts, all in a circular compound.

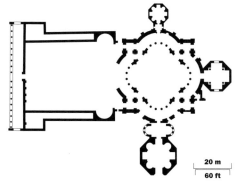

20 m
60 ft

74 **Milan, S Lorenzo** c. 380, plan.

A palatine chapel originally, this major landmark was
apparently inspired by the octagonal palatine chapel of
Antioch – at least as a double-skinned, centralised structure
providing a continuous ambulatory and upper gallery. It is,
however, basically square and the projection of exedrae
from the sides recalls the triclinium of Hadrian's Villa
(see 17, page 48) – though there were only three in that place
of imperial epiphany. The identification of secular power
with the divine could hardly be clearer. Variations on the
form distinguish several 6th-century Syrian churches.

The domed octagonal structure attached to the south,

75 **Milan, S Lorenzo** interior.

now dedicated to S Aquilino, was probably originally intended as an imperial mausoleum. It recalls the form of the entrance pavilion to Hadrian's Piazza d'Oro (see 21, page 53) and, beyond that, the garden rooms of the Domus Augustana on the Roman Palatine (see 11, pages 32–33).

The original conception of the square space surrounded by two-storeyed semi-domed exedrae was respected in the rebuilding carried out towards the end of the 16th century under the direction of Martino Bassi – though the present piers replaced columns.

Roman palaces were adopted for palatine chapels. The double-skinned quatralobe – as in the throne room of the Piazza d'Oro complex in Hadrian's Villa (see 20, page 52) was preferred in many parts of the empire, from northern Italy to Syria. The grandest of these, the Milanese church now dedicated to S Lorenzo, had galleries and was preceded by a triumphal entrance screen (fastigium).[74-76]

After the example set by Constantine in the Church of the Holy Apostles in Constantinople, basilica and martyrium were combined to enshrine the column of St Simeon at Qalat-Siman on a scale that ceded little to the imperial prototype.[77-78] Fully in accordance with the Syrian tradition, there was a triumphal

76 **Milan, S Lorenzo** exterior from original entrance.

An atrium, now largely vanished, was entered through a fastigium which descends through the Palace of Diocletian (see 47, page 113) at least from the motif applied to the Arch of Tiberius at Orange (see volume 3, IMPERIAL FORM, page 227). The 16th-century refurbishment preserved the towers of the original which possibly buttressed a central groin vault. This was crowned by a fifth square tower in place of the present dome and its octagonal drum.

77 Qalat-Siman, monastery church of St Simeon Stylites c. 480, view from the south.

The south narthex had a grand entrance in the form of a triumphal arch in accordance with a tradition, strong in Syria and the Levant, of endowing the precincts of temples with propylaea.

78 OVERLEAF **Qalat-Siman, church and monastery of St Simeon Stylites.**

Though doubtless modelled on Constantine's Church of the Holy Apostles in Constantinople, this extraordinary combination of basilica and martyrium has a central octagon in place of the square of the prototype. Originally roofed with timber, if roofed at all over the saint's column rising from its centre, it is joined by four aisled basilicas to form a huge cross 90 metres (295 feet) long on the east–west axis, 80 metres (260 feet) north–south. There were narthexes to the west and south; apses terminate nave and aisles at the east end. Mouldings are somewhat wayward: in particular architraves rise unbroken from the horizontal to curve up over arches, and the acanthus of incomplete Corinthian capitals are windswept into asymmetry. However, in monumentality and even classicism, this great church eclipsed all its contemporaries.

79 Ravenna, so-called Tomb of Galla Placidia 424.
In fact accommodating the remains of the Emperor
Honorius as well as those of his sister and her husband,
this small building is not quite centralised – the northern
arm, connecting with S Croce, extends beyond the length
of the others. Cross-shaped martyria were not uncommon
in northern Italy and the form was to become extremely
important in the churches of the east.

entrance worthy of an emperor. On a tiny scale, centralisation was adapted to the imagery of the cross in the so-called Tomb of Galla Placidia at Ravenna.[79] The patroness' brother, the Emperor Honorius, having lost Rome and the mausoleum projected for him beside S Pietro in Vaticano, was also buried here below the dome at the crossing. A cross of equal arms, approximated here, is called a Greek cross in distinction from the Latin cross of the elongated basilica.

80 **Ravenna, S Vitale** mosaic.

The Emperor Justinian and Empress Theodora offer gifts in the presence of Archbishop Maximian, under whom the church was consecrated after 546.

The centralised form of the Greek cross was the key to the evolution from the basilica of a church type specifically designed to cater for eastern ritual: it transformed the nave bay before the sanctuary which, partitioned from the transepts for the use of the clergy, had hitherto approximated a square (see 72, page 181). The credit for this is probably due to architects of Justinian[80] working on the rebuilding of Hagia Eirene[81] in Constantinople after its destruction in the Nike riots of 532 – though there is some doubt about their initial conception. The rebuilding of the great basilica of St John the Evangelist at Ephesus furthered the process: it was a Latin cross building with a dome each over the sanctuary, transepts and crossing and two domed bays forming the nave.[82]

The greatest exercise involving the interpolation of a domed cross into a longitudinal envelope was the stupendous Church of the Holy Wisdom (Hagia Sophia), the principal glory of the Byzantine east at the heart of the imperial capital, also built by Justinian following the devastation of the Nike riots. First, however, Justinian was responsible for SS Sergius and Bacchus in Constantinople[83] and for the completion of S Vitale in Ravenna.[84-85]

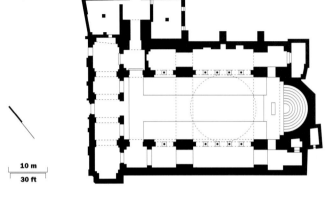

81 **Constantinople, Hagia Eirene** begun shortly after
532, reconstructed mid 8th century, plan and section.

Begun, like Hagia Sophia, immediately after its
predecessor was destroyed in the Nike riots, Hagia Eirene
was remodelled after an earthquake in 740. Analysis of the
materials and their usage demonstrates that much of the
basilican substructure and the domed crossing is original
though extensively repaired after a fire in 564. As there
were then unvaulted trabeated galleries above the aisles,

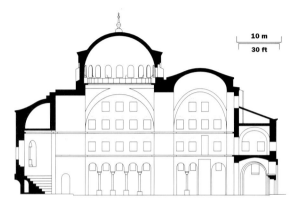

their ends still surviving embedded in later masonry, it is hard to imagine how the dome was buttressed unless there were lateral as well as longitudinal barrel vaults above the roofs of the galleries.

The earliest-known precedent for the domed basilica has been detected in S Thekla at Meriamlik in Cilicia (c. 480). In Constantinople the earliest-known example of a domed church is S Polyeuktos (524).

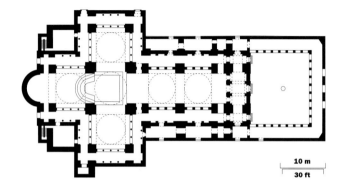

82 **Ephesus, St John the Evangelist** founded 450,
rebuilt under Justinian between c. 540 and 565, plan.

A standard aisled basilica was transformed into
a complex of six domes, one each over the sanctuary,
crossing and transept arms, two slightly elliptical ones
over the nave. Pendentives effected the transition from
square to circle and the lunettes over the galleries of
the nave bays were walled and doubtless pierced with
slender windows.

83 OVERLEAF **Constantinople, SS Sergius and Bacchus**
begun before 527, plan and section.

Begun by Justinian as a chapel associated with the palace
he occupied as heir to the throne, SS Sergius and Bacchus
was completed early in the 530s. It was interposed on an
awkward site between the palace and the new basilica
of SS Peter and Paul, communicating with each through
galleries at both levels. Hence the conception: a domed
octagon, forming a canopy over the prince's private
worship, encapsulated in a square, with space between
the two for the galleries of communication. The eight piers
carrying the dome frame alternately straight and semi-
circular colonnades which support the upper gallery and
screen ambulatory from nave at both levels – except to the
east where an apsidal projection provides the sanctuary.

The influence of works like the so-called Temple of
Minerva Medica in Rome (see 12, pages 36–37) may well be
seen in the design of the central octagon, but precedents
for its encapsulation in a rectangle are harder to find.
Krautheimer is surely right in recalling, primarily,
Eusebius' description of the so-called Golden Octagon
built by Constantine as a palatine chapel in Antioch (now
completely obliterated): the octagonal main space, golden-
domed possibly from the outset, had exedrae and was

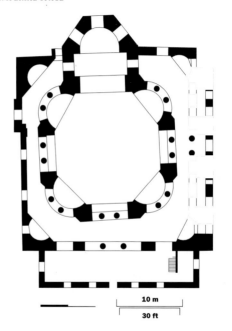

10 m

30 ft

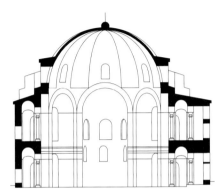

encapsulated in a colonnaded ambulatory and galleries.
Elsewhere double-skinned quatralobe plans are not
uncommon, S Lorenzo in Milan (see 74, page 184) being
one of the grandest. Similar forms are to be found in the
Balkans, Anatolia and Armenia and were popular in Syria.
Behind all these, of course, is the simple idea of ringing
a centralised space with a columned ambulatory – as in
S Costanza (see 66, page 170).

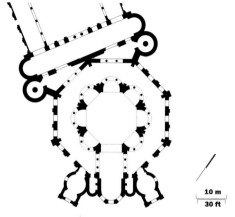

10 m
30 ft

84 **Ravenna, S Vitale** plan and section.

Commissioned by Bishop Ecclesius (521–32) and
probably begun just before his death, S Vitale was not
completed much before the death of Bishop Victor
(538–45). The atrium precedes the oddly tangential
narthex, separated from the main body of the building by
wedge-shaped vestibules neither of which opens the main
axis. Beyond, octagon is inscribed in octagon, unlike the
scheme evolved for SS Sergius and Bacchus, but as circle

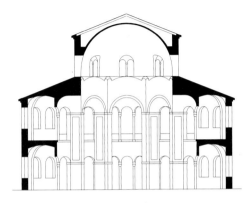

10 m
30 ft

was ringed by circular ambulatory for S Costanza (see 66, page 170). As in SS Sergius and Bacchus, there is a gallery level, but here all eight arches supporting the central dome frame semi-circular exedrae except to the east, where the ambulatory is interrupted by a square chancel before the sanctuary apse. Regularity of rhythm has been preferred to alternation and the proportions have been corrected to the advantage of the verticals. The relatively open site allowed more windows to admit much more light.

Unlike either Hagia Eirene or Hagia Sophia, SS Sergius and Bacchus and S Vitale are essentially rationalist compositions. Each demonstrates the appeal and limitation of rationalism in church architecture: the central space is octagonal, with eight great arches supporting the dome and semi-circular recessions with galleries on either side of the main axis, but what determines the entrance and where is the altar to be if not below the dome in the centre? As all the sides are equal, the location of the entrance can only be determined pragmatically – on the line of access – or by convention: on the axis of prayer facing east. If the clergy are to be separated from the laity, pragmatism likewise dictates the projection of a sanctuary out opposite the entrance.

85 **Ravenna, S Vitale** interior.

The pavement, columns and associated revetment of imported marble remain from the original campaign of work on the interior. Begun in 546, this also included the rare and important pre-iconoclastic mosaics which embellish the chancel (see 80, page 194). The 18th-century frescoes mask the octagonal umbrella vault and the squinches used instead of pendentives to support it.

Hagia Sophia

Hagia Sophia[86] may be seen as a basilica with apse, nave and aisles, narthex and atrium, but it is also a Greek cross in which the western and eastern arms have been rounded off to provide great hemicycles.[87] Unlike the greatest of Roman domes, those of the Pantheon (see 6, page 18) or the calidarium of the Baths of Caracalla (see 25, pages 64–65), which rest on cylindrical walls, Hagia Sophia's dome covers a square. As we have seen, a polygonal subsidiary chamber of the Caracalla complex (see 26, page 66) was domed, and where the dome's circumference diverged from the plane of the arches supporting it, Caracalla's architect inserted pendentives. The so-called Temple of Minerva Medica (see 12, pages 36–37) in Rome followed this precedent. S Vitale in Ravenna (see 84, pages 202–03) had both squinches and fragmentary pendentives but in SS Sergius and Bacchus (see 83, pages 200–01) the oblique angles of the octagon are continued as groins. At Hagia Eirene (see 81, pages 196–97) the same technique was used over a square where the four central arches provided much less support. In adapting this strategy to the monumental scale of Hagia Sophia, the achievement of Justinian's architects, Anthemius of Tralles and Isidorus of Miletus, was prodigious: even with the once-dazzling mosaics drastically depleted, their dome seems immaterial, like the canopy of heaven borne only by seraphim.[88]

Despite the unprecedented scale, Anthemius and Isidorus took only five years to build Hagia Sophia (532–37). Subsequent problems in sustaining the dome were due as much to earthquake as to miscalculation. Remedial buttressing measures explain in part the extraordinary, pragmatic approach to the exterior – the organic build-up of forms in response to

86 OVERLEAF **Constantinople, Hagia Sophia (Church of the Holy Wisdom)** 532, with Hagia Eirene (right).

The main basilica of Constantine's capital, seat of the patriarch and palatine chapel was dedicated only in 360. Rebuilt after a fire in 404, it was destroyed in the Nike riots of 532. Justinian immediately decided to rebuild it on an unprecedented scale. His engineer-architects, Anthemius of Tralles and Isidorus of Miletus, oversaw the achievement of the stupendous work in five years and the church was consecrated on 27 December 537. The principal church of eastern Christendom, it was converted to a mosque immediately after the fall of Constantinople to the Ottoman Turks on 29 May 1453.

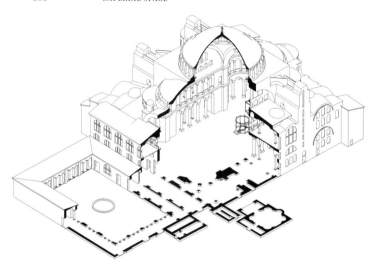

87 **Constantinople, Hagia Sophia** cutaway axonometric and worm's-eye view axonometric (OVERLEAF).

Inscribed in a rectangle about 70 by 75 metres (220 by 250 feet) were a square – 100 Byzantine feet or just over 31 metres (102 feet) per side – and two semi-circles flanked by twin series of smaller squares and rectangles. An extrusion of the SS Sergius and Bacchus scheme (see 83, pages 200–01), the plan thus resembles a basilica but with a square nave, two apses and sub-divided aisles. Some 55 metres (180 feet) high, four arches carry a huge dome with the aid of the most monumental pendentives ever conceived. The central arches spring from four great piers whose buttresses to the north and south, great masses of masonry capped with little towers, impose the major divisions between the groin-vaulted aisle chambers. Not to the degree intended, perhaps, east–west buttressing is provided by the semi-domed hemicycles which form the two huge apses. Semi-circular exedrae punctuate their perimeters, as in SS Sergius and Bacchus and S Vitale (see 84, pages 202–03), leaving piers to frame the entrance from the western atrium and the apsidal sanctuary at the east end.

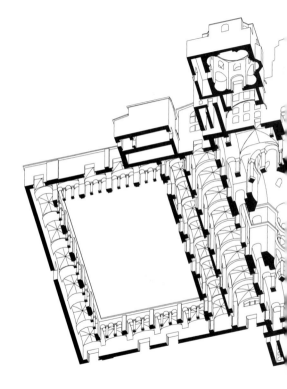

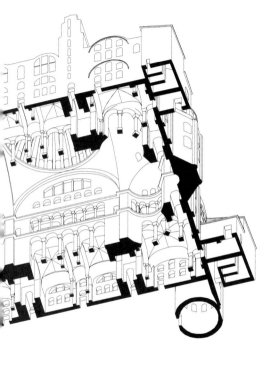

structural necessity rather than aesthetic principle,
which seems so overwhelmingly impressive to the
post-functionalist eye. Here, in fact, is the apotheosis
of interior architecture, of spatial architecture: in
antithesis to the antique temple and the stamping of
form with the order of the gods, this is the construction of space as the prelude to heaven.

Contemporary writers liken the dome of Hagia
Sophia to the vault of heaven: its supporting arches
mark the cardinal directions of space, its piers and
pavement the mountains and plains of earth. The
patriarch and clergy, whose hierarchy reflects that of
the angels, represent heaven and in their ceremonial
evoke the spiritual world of the resurrected Christ.
They performed the most sacred part of their office,
the celebration of the Eucharist, behind the curtains of

88 Constantinople, Hagia Sophia interior from the west.
Many different-coloured marbles were brought from the
furthest reaches of the empire and beyond for the columns
of the nave arcades and exedrae, entablatures, the revetment
of the walls, and the pavement: green Thessalian marble was
used for the nave columns, red porphyry (possibly recycled)
for the lower storey of the exedrae, and white Proconnesian

marble (from the imperial quarries on the islands of the
Sea of Marmara) for the shafts of the columns of aisles
and galleries. Smaller in the upper levels, the columns
were increased in number and set closer together, to some
discordance with those below, perhaps in modification of
the original design. Bronze bands protect the main shafts
from splitting and capitals incorporate impost blocks now
that columns regularly support arches.

The vaults and domes were covered in mosaics, now
mainly lost or obscured. The windows were glazed in
various colours, grading the quality of light from the sombre
aisles to the relatively bright nave, but the original effect is
difficult to recapture since the blinding of many openings
to reinforce the structure. The focus has been lost with
the original, sumptuously furnished sanctuary and the
deflection of the main axis to establish the direction of
Mecca for the orientation of Muslim prayer. The order of
repeated squares and circles and the regular sequence of
three, five and seven elements is certainly apparent, but here
too the original impact is masked by later interventions –
not least the huge Muslim discs inscribed with the names of
God. However, as the outer envelope bears no developed
relationship to its main content, many of the subsidiary
spaces are residual, and viewed through their screening

columns even the pure geometry of the main spaces was always denied.

Behind the sumptuous skin, the novelty of Justinian's achievement – a huge dome floating high over a cubical space – depended on the use of brick as much as on the exploitation of the pendentive principle. The eight great piers are built of stone; the walls are of brick reinforced with courses of limestone; an incredibly thin, hence light, layer of brick set in thick mortar forms the vaults. Like the plan, this too was anticipated at SS Sergius and Bacchus. New, however, and of seminal importance, are the flying buttresses which transmit the thrust of the western arcades to piers reinforcing the wall of the outer narthex, facing the missing atrium.

For all their celebrated command of physics, the architects miscalculated the buttressing of the relatively shallow, saucer-shaped dome: the piers and arches supporting it soon began to splay outwards and the dome fell through in 558. The arches and piers were strengthened and the expanse of void reduced within the great lunettes to the north and south as enhanced support for the steeper ribbed dome completed in 563. Support for this was augmented in the 9th century with flying buttresses but it collapsed partially in 989 and again in 1346.

the screened chancel to the great eastern apse where they appeared to read the scriptures.

The emperor and his entourage establish the earthly equivalent of the heavenly hierarchy, the emperor ranking with the apostles and even re-enacting Christ's institution of the Eucharist at the most elevated state banquets. The emperor entered Hagia Sophia with the patriarch, was even admitted to the sanctuary, but witnessed the service in the main from the imperial enclosure in the aisle chamber to the right of the great western apse through which he processed. Communion was brought by patriarch to emperor at the eastern edge of the nave. Together in this unique church, at once cathedral and palatine chapel, emperor and patriarch represented the dual nature of Christ. And the Christian empire was dependent upon their conjunction, effected in the great ceremony of the imperial mass, for which the bi-apsidal space was devised, and made manifest under the central dome.

Consolidation of form

A centralised space, crowned by a dome representing heaven, came to be seen as the ideal theatre for the performance of the mystery of the Eucharist, and the form was generally adopted for churches in the east.[89] The realisation of this idea with the increasingly rigorous co-ordination of square and circle, aspiring to the perfect geometry of the city of God, may be traced throughout the Byzantine world and on into the lands occupied by the Slav inheritors of Byzantine civilisation.

89 OVERLEAF **Mistra, Brontocheion monastery** early 14th century, view with the domed octagonal crossing of Hagia Theodoroi (c. 1290) to the right and the five-domed Hodegetria (c. 1310) in the background.

  The expression of the five domes of the cross-in-square structure was to be the norm in later Byzantine architecture, especially in the lands of the Slavs. Brick was the most common building material in Rome and Constantinople, indeed in the rump of the empire left after the Arab invasions. In Greece (as often in Rome), courses of stone reinforced the brickwork, and by the 10th century the two materials were often combined to decorative effect (as at Mistra). Geometric patterns emerged from a more-or-less random approach and where stone predominated, the blocks were framed by bricks on the cloisonné principle.

The origin of the cross-shaped church with a central dome and four smaller domed spaces in the corners is obscure – though it is to be found buried in the domed basilica (see 81, pages 196–97). Square in square, it is also implicit in the double-skin building. The centuries after Justinian saw the proliferation of double-skin plans, usually quatralobe in quatralobe, sometimes for martyria, sometimes for palatine chapels or even cathedrals. As to the Greek cross element of works like Hagia Eirene, those centuries also saw the transformation of a confined volume, closed to the corners, into the canonical regular quincunx in which space flows from the central square into the cross-arms and around piers or columns to squares in the corners. Far too little survives for the process to be traced comprehensively, though the achievement of the essential square geometry may have been assisted by work in the secular field – even going back to the Parthians through the palaces, if not the fire temples, of the Sassanians.

The 8th-century Koimesis church of Nicaea (Isnik),[90] with its dominant central domed space and subordinate domed corners, is a major landmark on the way to the evolution of the canonical quincunx

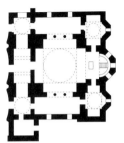

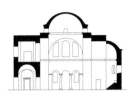

10 m

30 ft

90 **Nicaea (Isnik), Koimesis church** early 8th century, plan and section.

This building, which survived until 1920, had four subsidiary spaces in the corners of the cross. Larger than their western counterparts, those to the east served the clergy in their preparations for mass and are known in the Byzantine world as pastophoria.

Contemporary, possibly earlier, the Hagia Sophia of Salonica has a domed crossing, with a western arm slightly longer than the others, and domed pastophoria stepped in from the perimeter, out of alignment with the cross-vaulted chambers to either side of the triple-domed narthex.

91 **Cappadocia, Elmali Kilise** view towards the sanctuary. Activity at the site continued for many centuries and though this example probably dates from the 11th century there are precise precedents for it among the works datable from their non-figurative frescoes to before the end of the iconoclastic period.

plan, though the geometry is still far from regular. Over the next century approximations are known elsewhere, and regularity seems to have been achieved by the second half of the 9th century in Constantinople, though the earliest examples of which much substance remains there are at least another half century later. Given the accidents of survival in an area often hostile to the Church after the Muslim invasion, it is possible that the earliest fully developed representative of the type may be found among the churches hewn from the limestone cliffs of Cappadocia in the early 9th or even late 8th century.[91] It is found earlier in the west, as we shall see.

Only after the 10th century does the quincunx form proliferate in Greece, the Balkans and the domains of the Slavs. By then basilican forms, simple halls and even the cross-domed type represented by the core of Hagia Eirene were long largely obsolete except on the primitive provincial level or, beyond, on the very periphery of Christendom. The great majority of later Byzantine churches and even cathedrals were associated with monasteries, and monastic communities, like parishes, were many and small. This was naturally reflected in the size of the churches, planned

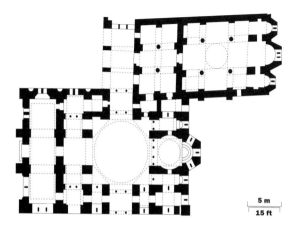

92 Hosios Lukas, Theotokos and Katholikon mid 10th and early 11th centuries respectively, plan of complex.

These adjoining churches well represent the simple quincunx plan of Greek cross in square and its expansion with the interpolation of a domed octagon wider than the arms of the cross. The Theotokos differs from the standard form only in the degree to which the sanctuary and

5 m

15 ft

93 **Daphne, Koimesis monastic church** c. 1080, interior of central dome.

The great dome is borne over its octagon on squinches, as at Hosias Lukas, but there are no galleries.

pastophoria project beyond the main square body of the building. Except to the east, the corner bays of the Katholikon's nave are blind though relieved with niches. The narthex and the upper corner bays of the nave have galleries, and bridges at the same level are carried across the transepts on arcades. In both works the apses are polygonal, as was usual in Greece, rather than semi-circular.

94 **Chios, Nea Moni Katholikon** mid 11th century, monastic complex and its enclosure.

95 **Chios, Nea Moni Katholikon** interior.

Founded by the Emperor Constantine IX Monomachos and built by imperial workmen sent from Constantinople, this church presumably represents an otherwise lost metropolitan type. A double narthex, the outer one domed over all three bays, the inner one domed only over the central bay, leads to the grand square nave. There are no transepts, but the piers supporting four great arches on each compactly on the consolidated quincunx. In addition to galleries for the laity, more space was occasionally achieved for the clergy by expanding the central dome to twice the width of the cross-arms or by erecting a domed sanctuary, larger than the crossing, beyond the eastern arm.[92–95]

In accordance with the liturgy of the eastern church as it had developed from Justinian's day, when the mystery of the Eucharist was celebrated in a curtained enclosure, the priests came out of the sanctuary to the naos for the reading of the scripture to the lay congregation crowded into the ancilliary spaces. This procedure prompted the development of the iconostasis, a screen erected between sanctuary and naos on which the holy icons were hung.[96] As the nave became the crossing in a centralised plan, it symbolised the world

side imply a Greek cross. Four smaller squinch-like arches link the main ones across the corners, transforming the square into an octagon at the base of the dome, though in fact the dome depends on pendentives. Contrary to usual Greek practice, but in accord with the metropolitan norm, the dome is segmental. The projecting sanctuary is flanked by square pastophoria in the usual way.

under heaven and was emblazoned accordingly with a hierarchy of images: Christ as the final judge (Pantocrator) or in Ascension in the dome; scenes from his life and Passion in the lunettes; the seraphim supporting the deity in heaven in the pendentives; the Virgin Mary in the apse of the sanctuary and episodes from her life elsewhere there. Art overcame architecture as it had not done before in the orbit of the Hellenes.

There were two media for masking the physical fabric of the church with these images – for obliterating this world with the glory to come – mosaic or fresco, according to the wealth of the foundation. A simple parish church like S Kliment at Ochrid made do with fresco.[97] Great metropolitan churches like those of Constantinople, ostentatious patrons like the founder of the Palermo Martorana[98] or rich abbeys like Daphne (see 93, page 227) or Nea Moni (see 95, page 230) indulged in mosaics. Assembled from myriad tiny pieces of glass backed by coloured enamel or gold leaf and laid in plaster inevitably at a slight angle to one

96 Patmos, monastery church of St John founded 1088, iconostasis (early 19th century with some earlier icons).

97 **Ochrid, S Kliment** late 13th century, interior showing vault frescoes.

98 **Palermo, Martorana** dedicated 1143, interior showing vault mosaics.

another, mosaic is unrivalled in reflecting the flickering light of candles to produce a shimmering, diaphanous veil, dematerialisng the enclosure – effecting its transfiguration into the empyrean.

Byzantium in the west

The Byzantine ideal, exported to Ravenna, was of lasting inspiration in northern Italy as well as in Sicily and the south – and in Venice above all. The standard basilica – together with other traditional early Christan building types[99] – was retained for the most important churches built in various parts of the lagoon at the head

99 **Florence, Baptistry** interior.

This great octagon was built on early Christian foundations and perhaps incorporates 6th- or 7th-century structure. The mosaics of the pavement and the umbrella vault were begun in the first quarter of the 13th century; later that century the vault was covered by a pyramidal roof and the original semi-circular apse was replaced with the present rectangular one. Apart from the mosaics, the chief treasures are the three sets of bronze doors – the southern ones by Andrea Pisano (1336), the northern and eastern ones by Lorenzo Ghiberti (1401).

101 **Torcello, cathedral** early 11th century and later, interior to the east.

100 **Florence, S Miniato** 1018 and later, exterior.

The panelling and blind arcading in black and white marble created a much more sumptuous effect than the early Christian norm and was a prime influence on the early Renaissance of Roman classicism. The division of the interior into three sections, with the sanctuary raised over a crypt, was also a departure from the basilican norm which was often to be followed – or paralleled – by Romanesque and gothic builders.

102 **Torcello, cathedral** apse with mosaic of the Virgin.

103 **Venice, S Marco (St Mark's)** founded 832, rebuilt
from 1063 and consecrated 1094, plan.

Reputedly responsible for converting the northern shore
of the Adriatic to Christianity, St Mark was also accredited
with the foundation of the see of Alexandria, whence his
remains were taken by the Venetians early in 828. The
original church built shortly thereafter to enshrine his relics
seems to have followed the Greek-cross precedent set by
Justinian's rebuilding of the Church of the Holy Apostles in
Constantinople and was later modified by raising the domes
over drums. The original church was restored after a fire
in 976 and rebuilt from 1063 on a scale of magnificence
reflecting the republic's conception of its standing as a
maritime power – especially *vis-à-vis* Constantinople.

Retaining some of the original structure, the 11th-century
rebuilding expanded and developed the initial conception,
carefully following the prototype even in such detail as the
design of the capitals. The nave was enlarged to exceed
the dimensions of the other arms in duplication of the
crossing – though in reality there is a slight discrepancy.
Whether there were originally masonry vaults throughout is
unknown though the precedent of five domes separated and
flanked by barrel vaults was well established. After 1204,
when the Venetians sacked Constantinople, the narthex was

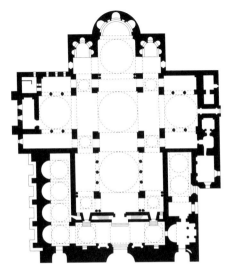

extended to the north and south sides to receive much of the
plunder and the baptistry installed in the south-west corner.
Much of the structure hidden by the rich revetment is of
poorly-laid brick-encased rubble. The domes are of brick
laid in concentric rings rather than radially as in the east.

of the Adriatic – as elsewhere in Italy.[100–102] The great metropolitan church of S Marco (St Mark's), enshrining the relics of its dedicatee and at once the cathedral of the Venetian archbishop and the palatine chapel of the doge, emulated the greatest achievements of Justinian in the combination of basilica, cross and dome.[103] In the lost spirit of Hagia Sophia, moreover, the structure is transformed by a complete set of mosaics within[104] and is celebrated in a mosaic portrait over the portal.[105] Nowhere are the physical realities of this world more triumphantly denied, and the image of the church as the image of the city of God – the *porta coeli* – more gloriously conveyed.

104 **Venice, S Marco** interior from the south transept. The vault mosaics were begun immediately after the structure was completed at the end of the 11th century, though work continued on them until the cycle was finished in the 18th century. The elimination of galleries over the aisles, allowing light in through the lateral barrel vaults, as in the renovation of Hagia Eirene in Constantinople (see 81, pages 196–97), and the piercing of the drums of the five main domes with windows, after

the example set by the renovators of the Church of
the Holy Apostles in Constantinople, enhanced the
effect of these mosaics immeasurably: bathed in light
they extend a diaphanous veil over the upper fabric
of the building, dissolving its mass and dissipating any
sense of physical constraint interposed between the
Christian soul and heaven. In carefully orchestrated
contrast, the lower zone, earthbound and reveted in
marble (largely from the second half of the 12th century)
remains dark.

105 **Venice, S Marco** portal mosaic of the translation of the remains of St Mark to the Venetian basilica.

The earliest mosaic to survive on the west front, this portrait of the church from that aspect post-dates 1204 since the horses pillaged then from Constantinople were already in place over the central portals.

After the sack of Constantinople by Venetian forces in 1204, S Marco was endowed with much pillaged treasure, including the bronze horses. The narthex was extended and the exterior remodelled, probably to celebrate the Venetian victory and to incorporate stolen marble. The profiles of the new work tend towards the oriental, in particular the slightly pointed arches. Originally expressed directly on the outside, the domes were covered by timber cupolas (again somewhat oriental in profile) in the 13th century and these seem to be shown here. However, as shown here the building has yet to undergo its final transformation in accordance with the florid taste of the later-Middle Ages.

glossary

ACANTHUS plant, stylised images of whose leaves are characteristic of CORINTHIAN CAPITALS.

AEDICULE ornamental pilastered niche to house a sacred image, for example.

AISLE side passage of a church or temple, running parallel to the NAVE and separated from it by COLUMNS or PIERS.

AMBULATORY semi-circular or polygonal arcade or walkway. (See page 170.)

APSE semi-circular domed or vaulted space, especially at one end of a BASILICA. Hence APSIDAL, in the shape of an apse.

ARCADE series of arches supported by COLUMNS, sometimes paired and covered so as to form a walkway.

ARCHITRAVE one of the three principal elements of an ENTABLATURE, positioned immediately above the CAPITAL of a COLUMN, and supporting the FRIEZE and CORNICE.

ATLANTE element in the shape of a male figure, used in place of a COLUMN.

ATRIUM inner court of a Roman house, usually unroofed at the middle, where the COMPLUVIUM allowed rainwater to collect in the IMPLUVIUM.

AULA REGIA public audience chamber in a royal or imperial court.

AXIS line used to establish geometry around which a building is designed. Hence, axial plan, in which the building is related to fundamental two- or three- dimensional base lines.

BALDACHINO canopy raised on columns over an altar or tomb, for example.

BAPTISTRY building dedicated to the rite of baptism.

BASILICA temple or other public building, consisting principally of a COLONNADED rectangular space enclosed by an AMBULATORY or having a central NAVE and side AISLES, and generally lit by a CLERESTORY. (See page 177.)

BAY one of a series of compartments of the interior of a building, the divisions being created by piers or columns, for example.

BELVEDERE open-sided roofed structure, freestanding or situated on the roof of a building so as to command a view.

BIT-HILANI columned PORTICO, specifically of 1st millennium BC Syria.

BUTTRESS support, usually stone, built against a wall to reinforce or take load.

CALIDARIUM hottest of the rooms in a Roman bath house.

CANOPY VAULT *see* VAULT, CANOPY.

CAPITAL top part of a COLUMN, supporting the ENTABLATURE. The part of the COLUMN which, taken together with the ENTABLATURE, forms the major defining element in the Greek ORDERS of architecture – DORIC, IONIC and CORINTHIAN.

CARDO road running north to south, later the principal longitudinal road of a town or city.

CARYATID female figure used as a support in place of a COLUMN.

CATACOMB burial place, usually in the form of a passageway with recessed side galleries for the disposition of cadavers.

CAVEA the seating within a theatre.

CENTRALISED PLAN design that is symmetrical in plan around the centre, allowing for reflection about both 90 and 180 degree axes.

CHANCEL part of a church where the clergy and choir are ranged, separated by a screen or railing from the main body of the building.

CIBORIUM canopy raised on columns so as to form a covering above an altar or tomb, for example.

CITADEL fortress, usually at the highest part of a town.

CLERESTORY windowed upper level providing light for a double-storey interior. (See page 183.)

CLOISONNÉ technique used in enamelling for dividing colours into different compartments.

CLOISTER covered ARCADE, often running around the perimeter of an open courtyard.

COFFERING decoration of a ceiling or VAULT with sunken rectangular or other polygonal panels.

COLONNADE line of regularly spaced COLUMNS.

COLUMN vertical member, usually circular in cross-section, functionally structural or ornamental or both, comprising a base, SHAFT and CAPITAL.

COMPLUVIUM rectangular opening above the centre of an ATRIUM, allowing rainwater to collect in the IMPLUVIUM.

COMPOSITE ORDER *see* ORDER, COMPOSITE.

CONCRETE building material composed of cement agglomerated with sand, gravel, stone chippings, et cetera.

CONSOLE support bracket, ornamental in form, with a curved outline.

CORINTHIAN ORDER *see* ORDER, CORINTHIAN.

CORNICE projecting moulding forming the top part of an ENTABLATURE.

COVE/COVING curved concave moulding forming or covering the junction between wall and ceiling.

CRYPT underground chamber, often beneath the CHANCEL of a church.

DADO the middle part, between base and CORNICE, of a PEDESTAL or the lower part of a wall when treated as a continuous pedestal.

DAIS raised platform, usually at one end of an internal space.

DECUMANUS road running east to west, later the main latitudinal road of a town or city.

DORIC ORDER *see* ORDER, DORIC.

DOUBLE-SKIN PLAN design in which the outer walls are echoed by inner walls or COLONNADES, leaving space between for an AMBULATORY, for example. (See page 184.)

ENTABLATURE part of the façade immediately above the COLUMNS,

usually composed of a supportive ARCHITRAVE, decorative FRIEZE and projecting CORNICE.

EXEDRA recess, usually APSIDAL, containing seats.

EXONARTHEX extension to the NARTHEX of a church, formed by the AISLES. (See page 182.)

FASTIGIUM a PEDIMENT or other structure in the shape of the gable end of a house, dignifying the entrance to a temple precinct or palace. (See page 113.)

FILIGREE decorative work formed from a mesh or by piercing material to give the impression of a mesh.

FLYING BUTTRESS an arch and more or less freestanding BUTTRESS which together take the load of a roof, for example.

FONT freestanding basin, usually of stone, for use in Christian baptism.

FORUM central open space of a town, usually a marketplace surrounded by public buildings.

FRESCO painting done on plaster which is not yet dry. (See page 234.)

FRIEZE the middle part of an ENTABLATURE, above the ARCHITRAVE and below the CORNICE, or more generally any horizontal strip decorated in RELIEF.

FRIGIDARIUM coolest of the rooms in a Roman bath house.

GALLERY upper storey projecting over the main space.

GROIN VAULT *see* VAULT, GROIN

HEMICYCLE semi-circular recessed structure on a grand scale.

HEROUM shrine dedicated to a demi-god or to the dead.

HIPPODROME arena for horse-racing and other sporting events

ICON image of a sacred subject, often acquiring sacred significance in its own right.

ICONOSTASIS screen separating the NAVE from the SANCTUARY in a Byzantine church, latterly used for placing ICONS. (See page 232.)

IMPLUVIUM rectangular tank in the middle of the ATRIUM of a Roman house for collecting rainwater.

IMPOST structural member – usually in the form of a MOULDING or block – at the top of a pillar, for example, on which an arch rests.

INTRADOS curve defined by the lower surface of an arch.

IONIC ORDER *see* ORDER, IONIC.

IWAN vaulted hall or recess opening off a court.

LARARIUM room in a Roman house used to contain images of the lares, the household gods.

LOGGIA a GALLERY open to the elements on one side.

LUNETTE semi-circular window or recess, usually at the base of a dome or vault.

MARTYRIUM shrine or chapel dedicated to Christian martyrs.

MAUSOLEUM tomb, usually of a dignitary, built on a grand scale.

MOSAIC decoration formed by embedding small coloured tiles or pieces of glass (TESSERAE) in cement. (See page 235.)

MOULDING the contour of a projecting or inset element.

NAOS main chamber of a temple, usually housing the cult statue.

NARTHEX chamber adjunct to the NAVE of a public building, usually a Christian church.

NATATIO swimming pool in a Roman bath house.

NAVE central body of principal interior

of, for instance, a church or temple.

NECROPOLIS cemetery, literally a
community of the dead.

OBELISK tall monolith of more or less
square cross-section, tapering towards
the top and ending in an integral
PYRAMID.

OCULUS circular window.

ORDER defining feature of classical
architecture, comprising a COLUMN
together with its ENTABLATURE.

ORDER, COMPOSITE hybrid order
embracing both IONIC and
CORINTHIAN elements in its CAPITAL.

ORDER, CORINTHIAN an evolution from
the IONIC ORDER, characterised by the
replacement of the CAPITAL VOLUTES
with a more elaborate and deeper
decorative arrangement.

ORDER, DORIC the oldest and most
simply functional of the three Greek
Orders of architecture, characterised
by a fluted and tapered COLUMN
without a base, topped by a plain
CAPITAL, surmounted by a relatively
high ENTABLATURE.

ORDER, IONIC slightly later and more
elaborate Order than the DORIC,
featuring fluted COLUMNS that have
bases and are topped by CAPITALS with
scrolled VOLUTES. The COLUMNS
typically are taller relative to their base
diameters than the DORIC, and are
correspondingly less acutely tapered.
The ENTABLATURE was less tall than
that of the DORIC, being originally
composed of ARCHITRAVE and
CORNICE only, though a FRIEZE
became usual later.

PALAESTRA public building for training
in athletics, typically smaller than a
gymnasium.

PARAPET low wall, usually for defensive
purposes.

PASTOPHERIA in the Byzantine church,
areas to the sides of the rear of the
sanctuary used by priests for
preparations for ritual. (See page 223.)

PEDESTAL base supporting for example
a COLUMN or statue.

PEDIMENT triangular area of wall,
usually a gable, above the
ENTABLATURE.

PENDENTIVE curved concave triangular
member used at the corners of a square
or polygonal structure so as to enable
reconciliation with a domed roof.
(See pages 67, 68.)

PERISTYLE row of COLUMNS surrounding a building or courtyard, or a courtyard so COLONNADED.

PIER supporting pillar for a wall or roof, often of rectangular cross-section.

PLINTH rectangular base or base support of a COLUMN or wall.

PODIUM continuous base or PEDESTAL consisting of PLINTH, DADO and CORNICE, to support a series of COLUMNS.

PORTA COELI gate of heaven.

PORTICO entrance to a building, featuring a COLONNADE.

PROPYLAEUM gateway, especially to a temple enclosure.

PYRAMID structure, usually of stone, with a square base and four triangular sides meeting in a point at the top.

QUADRIGA chariot drawn by four horses abreast.

QUATRALOBE area composed of four interlocking circular segments.

QUINCUNX structure composed of an agglomeration of five elements, four being identical and disposed to form more or less a hollow square, its centre being filled by the fifth. (See page 226.)

RAKING CORNICE an inclined CORNICE,

deployed above the TYMPANUM of a PEDIMENT.

RAMPART defensive earthwork, usually surrounding a fortress or citadel, often with a stone PARAPET.

RELIEF carving, typically of figures, raised from a flat background usually by cutting away more (HIGH RELIEF) or less (LOW RELIEF) of the material from which they are carved. (See page 92.)

REVETMENT decorative reinforced facing for a retaining wall.

RIB raised band on a vault or ceiling.

ROTUNDA circular room or building, usually with a domed roof.

SACRISTY room in a church for storing valuable ritual objects.

SANCTUARY the most sacred part of a church or temple, often where the altar is situated.

SCENAE FRONS flat wall forming the back of the stage in a semi-circular Roman theatre.

SHAFT more or less cylindrical element of a COLUMN rising from the base to the CAPITAL.

SQUINCH arch placed across the corner of a square structure so as to form a polygon capable of being roofed by a dome. (See page 32.)

STADIUM enclosed unroofed area for the performance of athletics.

STOA extended PORTICO or roofed structure with COLONNADE.

STUCCO type of plaster, especially used where decoration is to be applied.

TEMPIETTO small temple.

TEPIDARIUM room of intermediate temperature in a Roman bath house.

TESSERA small tile made of marble or glass used to form MOSAIC.

TETRAPYLON four columns surmounted by a PLINTH, or monumental arch with intersecting passages, used to mark the junction of major roads in a Roman town.

THERMAE public baths.

THOLOS dome, either freestanding or forming the centre of a circular building.

TRABEATED structurally dependent on rectilinear POST and BEAM supports.

TRANSEPT part of a large public/religious building that crosses the NAVE at right angles.

TRAVERTINE light-coloured limestone.

TRICLINIUM dining-room or principal reception room in a Roman house.

TYMPANUM triangular area of a PEDIMENT enclosed by CORNICES above and ENTABLATURE below; an area, usually recessed, formed by a LINTEL below and an arch above.

TUMULUS ancient burial mound.

VAULT structure forming an arched roof over a space.

VAULT, DOMICAL enclosing a more or less hemispherical space.

VAULT, BARREL enclosing a more or less hemicylindrical space.

VAULT, CANOPY creating a roof for a niche or tomb.

VAULT, GROIN enclosing a space composed of two intersecting, more or less hemicylindrical, shapes.

VERANDAH roofed COLONNADE attached to one or more sides of a building.

VESTIBULE courtyard in front of the entrance to a Greek or Roman house; hallway to a building; space adjunct to a larger room.

VILLA Roman country house.

VOLUTE scroll or spiral ornamental and/ or support member, characteristic of IONIC CAPITALS.

VOUSSOIR wedge-shaped stone deployed

in building an arch. Hence voussoir
arch where such stones are used.

ZIGGURAT building composed of a
stepped series of concentric rectangles,
the whole forming a truncated
pyramidal structure.

The books listed below are those the author found particularly useful as sources of general information on the architecture covered in this volume.

Boethius, A, *The Golden House of Nero*, Michigan 1960

Colledge, M A R, *Parthian Art*, London 1977

Davies, J, *The Origin and Development of Early Christian Church Architecture*, London 1952

Ghirshman, R, *Iran: Parthians and Sassanians*, London 1962

Grabar, A, *Martyrium*, 2 volumes, Paris 1943–46

Herzfeld, E, *Iran in the Ancient East*, Oxford 1941

Krautheimer, R, *Early Christian and Byzantine Architecture*, Harmondsworth 1965, revised 1986

MacDonald, W L, *Early Christian and Byzantine Architecture*, New York 1962

MacDonald, W L, *The Architecture of the Roman Empire*, 2 volumes, New Haven 1965 and 1986

Mango, C, *Byzantine Architecture*, New York 1976

Mathews, T F, *The Early Churches of Constantinople: Architecture and Liturgy*, University Park and London 1971

Mathews, T F, *The Byzantine Churches of Istanbul. A Photographic Survey*, University Park and London 1975

Smith, B, *Architectural Symbolism of Imperial Rome and the Middle Ages*, New York 1978

Smith, E B, *The Dome: A Study in the History of Ideas*, Princeton 1950

Ward-Perkins, J B, *Roman Architecture*, New York 1977

Ward-Perkins, J B, in D Talbot Rice, ed, *The Great Palace of the Byzantine Emperors*, Edinburgh 1958

bibliography

index

Figures in bold refer to the text; those in
ordinary type refer to captions; and
those in ordinary type with an asterisk
refer to illustrations.